SO-DNJ-168

Emergency Management In The States

The
Council of
State
Governments

Emergency Management in the States

By
Edward D. Feigenbaum
and
Mark L. Ford

ISBN-0-87292-052-6
Price: $10.00
RM-738

Much of the material in this publication was developed under a contract to the Federal Emergency Management Agency. Dr. Charles M. Girard and Dr. Paul Watson of FEMA's National Emergency Training Center and Assemblyman David D. Nicholas of Nevada were extremely helpful in supervising work under this contract.

Contents

Foreword

Each day states are threatened by different hazards, ranging from those caused by man and our ever-increasing technological manipulations to the unforeseen and often unpreventable havoc of nature. States that are prepared to cope with disasters inevitably fare better in protecting people and property, and in recovering more rapidly. For longer-term emergencies states must be even better equipped. Procedures must be planned, responsibilities defined and delegated, and authority exercised.

The Council of State Governments has long been interested in emergency management. The Council's Suggested State Legislation Committee was formed in 1941 to develop wartime emergency legislation, and it was the Council's 1959 continuity of government legislation that served as the basis for much of the existing statutory authority in the area. The State Disaster Act of 1972 and several CSG studies highlighted the Council's activity in emergency management during the past decade. Now with this compilation of state emergency management statutes, states can assess their relative emergency management capabilities.

Carl W. Stenberg
Executive Director

Introduction

Emergency management is the Rodney Dangerfield of state priorities: in competition with education, highway repair funding, public assistance, budget deficits and similar agenda items, it "just don't get no respect"—or at least the respect it deserves. Emergency management is no longer oriented toward "hard hat" civil defense, as once was the case throughout the country, nor does it consist of only relocation programs to meet the event of nuclear attack. Today, emergency management is an integrated, all-hazards approach to preparedness, mitigation, response and recovery from a broad spectrum of both natural and technological hazards. In spite of offering this comprehensive approach to critical problems, emergency management is not typically foremost in the minds of the electorate, and this absence of public interest perpetuates legislative and administrative complacence.

Because emergency management issues tend to attract scant public interest and evoke even less public debate, little tends to be done to improve state emergency management capabilities until there is a stimulus—a major emergency or incident—that alerts the public and public officials to flaws, gaps and other inadequacies in the system. The government response, then, tends to be reactive rather than proactive, and reactive planning is unlikely to be comprehensive. Rather, the response is typically only sufficient to meet the immediate problem, and does not fulfill the needs of an all-hazards, integrated emergency management system. A state may be adequately equipped to handle exactly the same emergency twice, but such an approach minimizes the likelihood that the state will be able to respond effectively to an emergency of even a slightly different nature.

Devoting resources to emergency management and preparedness is, to an extent, akin to buying insurance. One never knows how much insurance is adequate. Indeed, most would agree that they pay too much for insurance—and never use it. Those who have had to rely on insurance benefits, however, will likely say that they wish that they had better coverage. Like insurance, emergency management capability and emergency preparedness are always too expensive until an incident mobilizes the system—and the public inevitably finds that the resources devoted to the task were grossly inadequate.

Money is not the panacea for emergency management programs. Emergency officials are likely to cite changed attitudes of government leaders as being as important as additional funding. Our modern technological society all but dictates that emergency management be considered as a basic function of government. Response to major incidents is apt to involve many local and state agencies (state police, fire marshal, health department, environ-mental/natural resources department, transportation/highway department, etc.) in addition to the designated lead emergency agency and the governor. The emergency agency must be recognized and accepted by other entities and officials as the proper authority, and must have sufficient power to call upon the resources of other agencies as needed. The ability to identify and marshal available resources may be more important than securing new or additional equipment and manpower. Good, ongoing working relationships among the principals are necessary, and these relationships are difficult to foster in an atmosphere that removes the emergency agency from the normal governmental routine.

Finally, public officials must be sensitive to the unique problems of emergency managers and emergency management, particularly officials who play a key role in developing the necessary statutory framework for emergency management. Definitions of emergencies in state statutes should account for all potential major hazards, and consonance with federal definitions may prove useful. Emergency plans should be developed, with clear assignments, contingency provisions, and outlines of *what* actions will be taken, supplemented with information on *how* these tasks will be implemented. Plans should be functional and take into account local needs and concerns. Legislative oversight of state agency emergency planning can help to ensure this. Provisions should be made to carry on the activities of government in the event of an emergency. These provisions should be both practical and, at best, take into consideration the constitutional and statutory backdrop for selection of officers. The circumstances compelling and the limits upon declarations of emergency should be elaborated. Delegation of authority should be clear, and an organizational structure concisely delineated. Liability and licensing requirements might deter qualified professionals from responding to emergencies, and altering these requirements in extraordinary circumstances should be afforded special consideration. Interstate compacts may prove to be useful tools for obtaining assistance in times of emergency, and the potential of creative interstate pacts should be examined closely, particularly by states with major metropolitan areas bordering on other states. Streamlined state procedures for applying for post-emergency federal assistance and formulas for equitable apportionment of financial responsibility in cases of emergencies caused by other than natural hazards should be considered.

Emergency Management in the States

Explanation of Categories and Areas for Future Consideration

This section provides background for the state legal summaries and offers additional material by which to evaluate the adequacy of state laws—at least on paper. One should recognize that the rhetoric of state laws and plans does not always reflect the operational reality of a state system.

Experience has shown that states with highly formalized, elaborately detailed procedures may choose not to follow them in times of emergency, while states that may be short on written guidelines often have developed informal response networks that, by virtue of long-time personal relationships among the principals and frequent activity, are efficient systems that meet the challenges posed by any given incident.

Definition:

• The definition outlines the circumstances under which a state of emergency may be proclaimed, following the language of the statute. Specific examples of "generic" emergencies—fire, flood, riot, etc.—are not included unless the state has included a unique example, such as an energy shortage, or plant infestation, or nuclear accident.

Items For Consideration

Not all states recognize all categories of emergencies that may be expected to arise. This lack of inclusion may result in delays in response and recovery. States must recognize that the technological hazards of today should be accounted for in planning. Experience has shown that a severe spill of a hazardous material in a major metropolitan area can prove to be even more deleterious than a significant flood, particularly when long-term effects are considered. Definitions of emergencies should, at a minimum, cover enemy attack, diseases and natural disasters, and man-made hazards.

Declaration of Emergency:

• It may be inferred that an emergency may be proclaimed only when the governor reasonably believes that the conditions outlined in a state's definition of emergency are realized.

• In states where the text stipulates that the legislature may terminate an emergency, the legislature may, by joint resolution, direct the governor to proclaim an emergency to be at an end.

Items For Consideration

Provisions for declarations of emergencies are relatively uniform across states, with the governor typically being afforded full discretion. Consideration should be given to allowing other officers to declare a state of emergency in the event of the absence, disability or death of a governor.

Procedures for termination of proclamations of emergencies vary widely across states. Some states have no formal procedure for termination of proclamations, others permit rescission by the governor at his or her discretion, and still others require legislative acquiescence to revoke the proclamation. Checks on the authority of the governor in the form of absolute time limitations for the duration of proclamations and legislative approval for continuance also are not consistent from state to state. States may wish to assess policies which give the governor complete authority in determining the duration of an emergency situation, and include firm but reasonable deadlines that allow the governor to adequately respond to emergencies before requiring further affirmative legislative action to continue disaster efforts.

Governor's Emergency Powers:

• Powers that the governor is universally afforded in emergencies, such as the power to evacuate a disaster area or to prohibit certain conduct in the area, are generally not elaborated in the summaries.

• Most states permit the governor to commandeer or use private property. These states usually direct the government to exhaust available state resources first before taking private property.

• A few states allow the governor to order conscription of private citizens into state emergency service. Citizens so conscripted are compensated for their services.

• States typically allow the governor to suspend all or parts of certain laws to some degree. Where the summary notes that a governor may suspend any statute regulating procedures for the conduct of state business, the provision does not affect private businesses in the state, but rather the procedures state agencies are normally required to follow. Administrative law refers to the rules, orders and regulations of state governmental agencies.

Items For Consideration

Most state governors acquire broad authority in times of emergency, usually without any significant restrictions. Such broad discretion is most often justified by the need for immediate centralized action and the inability of larger groups such as advisory councils or legislatures to assemble soon after an emergency has occurred. Attention may be devoted to determining rational time re-

2

straints for the use of such broad authority, outside of the realm of legislative termination of emergency proclamations, perhaps allowing unfettered powers to be exercised until an advisory council, legislative unit or the full legislature is able to meet.

Lead Agency:

• Each state has established an administrative agency with primary responsibility for emergency planning. Where the governor is statutorily required to develop a state emergency program, the duty is delegated to such an agency. Slightly more than one-half of the lead disaster preparedness agencies are affiliated with civil defense or state military offices.

• State emergency planning agencies are in charge of preparing state disaster plans and also often create, coordinate and implement city and county disaster plans as well. All such plans are embraced here in the term "state emergency program."

• Some states have established advisory councils to assist the governor in emergency management during a crisis. The boards sometimes are mandated to meet periodically and perform other planning tasks. The members of these councils usually serve at little or no salary, although their expenses are paid.

Mutual Aid Agreements:

• Membership in the Interstate Civil Defense and Disaster Compact is noted. The compact is not a national agreement to which all the states are members, but rather is a form of agreement that authorizes a state to enter into bilateral or multilateral agreements with its neighbors.

Items For Consideration

The Interstate Civil Defense and Disaster Compact, developed in the early 1950s, has been enacted in most states but with considerable variation in approach as to participants. Some states have enacted the Compact with all other jurisdictions eligible to join, others only with their bordering states, and still others with only certain bordering states. There has been no real effort in the past 25 years to clear up this schizophrenic pattern of enactment. However, it is now becoming increasingly clear that there must be more effective interjurisdictional coordination to meet the growing disaster problem. The Compact provides an invaluable legal basis for interstate and possible state-foreign relationships that are useful to the proper functioning of a comprehensive disaster preparedness and response system. One section provides specifically for the enactment of the Compact with all bordering states and gives the governor authority to enter into the Compact with other appropriate states as well. The Council of State Governments' Committee on Suggested State Legislation has noted that it is vital that this provision be enacted by all states.

Public/Personal Liability:

• Where a summary notes that persons are generally immune from liability, this means that they are not generally chargeable for negligence, but that they may be held responsible for gross negligence and intentional misconduct.

• Most states have a statute essentially providing that any person who controls real estate or premises and who voluntarily and without compensation licenses such property for use as shelter during an emergency or during emergency training exercises (and his or her estate and successors in interest) is not liable for death or injury occurring on the property when it is used for emergency purposes. Since the language is almost always the same, only significant differences in such a statute are noted here.

Items For Consideration

Several states have, during their most recent legislative sessions, enacted legislation immunizing public entities or public safety employees acting within the scope of their employment from liability for an injury caused by their actions in abating hazards, unless performed in bad faith or in a grossly negligent manner. Immunity has also been granted in similar circumstances for uncompensated persons, firms or corporations rendering assistance or advice in mitigating hazards, if it is not their duty to do so.

Statutes that assign or apportion financial responsibility for causing or perpetuating emergencies (such as hazardous materials spills) can ease the financial burden of response and mitigation for the responding jurisdiction.

Licensing Requirements:

• If the state allows for suspension of licensing requirements, this is noted. States that have entered into the Interstate Civil Defense and Disaster Compact with other states are covered under Article IV of the Compact, which allows professionals licensed in other states to practice in the affected state during an emergency.

Continuity of Government:

• Where a state provides for emergency interim succession, the successors are considered to be temporary until "normal" procedures for filling vacancies can be used.

• Where multiple successors are designated, the individual at the top of the list succeeds to the office.

• Generally, an emergency successor to an officer in line to succeed the governor may not, in turn, succeed the governor during the emergency.

While most states allow for the suspension of state licensing requirements in times of emergency, many do not. Although it seems unlikely that a state would actually prosecute a good samaritan for practicing without a state license, a professional might be deterred from rendering aid by the possibility of liability in tort. The waiver of license requirements in an emergency should be provided for by law.

Items For Consideration

A few states have special emergency interim succession provisions allowing vacancies in offices to be filled rapidly and with a minimum of confusion and controversy; several other states make no such allowances. The latter states often rely upon non-emergency procedures for filling vacancies caused by death or disability, which, as can be seen from a review of the statutes and constitutions, are often cumbersome, time-consuming and require the deliberation of groups of key individuals or officials who may be unable to assemble rapidly in order to perform the necessary work. Often gubernatorial vacancies are filled by legislative action and legislative vacancies filled by action taken by local officials who themselves may never have been selected through a public election. Streamlining succession procedures should be considered and thought devoted to provisions that require emergency interim successors to be designated from among individuals who formerly held the position in question. Texas, for example, passed a constitutional amendment in late 1983 providing for interim emergency succession. The amendment's sponsor proposed that retired legislators be the first tapped under the system.

Finally, the question of the continuation of normal functions of government in times of emergency should be foremost in the minds of those considering continuity of government legislation. The chances of having an emergency of several weeks' duration raises the issue of provision of essential services. For example, how will public assistance funds or food stamps be distributed? Elections may also be disrupted, even if an emergency is short-lived, as may be the case with a tornado or hurricane. Proper planning is the key for smooth operation of government in times of disaster.

Alabama

Title 31, Chapter 9

DEFINITION: The Alabama Emergency Management Act of 1955 covers disasters or emergencies of unprecedented size and destructiveness resulting from hostile action or natural causes.

DECLARATION OF EMERGENCY: An emergency may be declared by proclamation of the Governor, or by joint resolution of the legislature, and may continue indefinitely until terminated by proclamation or joint resolution. If the Governor declares a state of emergency management emergency, s/he must call the legislature into session.

GOVERNOR'S EMERGENCY POWERS: The government may, during an emergency, procure materials and facilities for emergency management without regard to the limitations of any existing law. Property seized, however, must be compensated for, and the Governor may not order the seizure of property owned by a newspaper company, nor the wire facilities leased or owned by news services.

LEAD AGENCY: The Emergency Management Agency is responsible for developing and carrying out a program for emergency management.

MUTUAL AID AGREEMENTS: The Governor is allowed to enter into mutual aid agreements with other states and neighboring foreign countries. Alabama is a member of the Interstate Civil Defense and Disaster Compact.

PUBLIC/PERSONAL LIABILITY: Persons who allow the use of their property as shelter during an emergency are generally immune from civil liability. Volunteers who act as emergency management workers are also generally immune from liability.

LICENSING REQUIREMENTS: The Governor may suspend license requirements for persons licensed in other states, as per ICDDC Article IV.

CONTINUITY OF GOVERNMENT: When the Governor appears to be of unsound mind, it is the duty of the Alabama Supreme Court, upon request in writing of any two officers named in Section 127 of the Constitution (Lieutenant Governor, President Pro Tempore of the Senate, Speaker of the House of Representatives, Attorney General, State Auditor, Secretary of State, State Treasurer) not next in succession to the office, to determine the Governor's mental condition. No provision is made, however, for determining the physical disability of the Governor. If the Governor is adjudged to be of unsound mind, the Alabama Supreme Court so decrees and files a copy of that decree in the office of the Secretary of State. The official next in line performs the duties of the office. If, when the time comes, the individual performing the duties of office denies that the Governor has been restored to his mind, the Supreme Court ascertains the truth. If the Court determines that the Governor has been restored to his or her mind, it files a duly certified copy of the decree with the Secretary of State.

Alabama's Emergency Interim Succession Act provides for mass vacancies in the legislature following an enemy attack. Each legislator must designate one or more qualified persons to succeed him during an emergency. There is no similar provision to fill executive and judicial offices.

Within 90 days of an enemy attack, the Governor shall convene the legislature at any place within or without the state if Montgomery is unsafe or inconvenient.

Alaska

DEFINITION: Alaska has two laws governing emergency management, the Civil Defense Act for emergencies resulting from enemy attack, sabotage, or other hostile action, and the Alaska Disaster Act which applies to natural and non-military manmade disasters.

DECLARATION OF EMERGENCY: The Governor may declare both types of emergency. A civil defense state of emergency may continue indefinitely. When the Governor proclaims a condition of disaster emergency, s/he must call a special session of the legislature to approve all actions taken by the Governor (the call for special session may be cancelled if the presiding officers of the Senate and the House unanimously agree to cancel). The legislature or Governor may terminate disaster emergency declaration at any time, but it may not last longer than 30 days unless renewed by the legislature.

GOVERNOR'S EMERGENCY POWERS: The Governor may suspend the provisions of any statutes regulatory of state business, and any administrative laws if necessary. The Governor is given authority to commandeer or utilize any private property, except for that of the news media, as necessary, provided that the owners are afforded full compensation.

LEAD AGENCY: The Alaska Division of Emergency Services is the unit of the Department of Military Affairs responsible for implementing the state disaster plan during a disaster emergency. During a civil defense emergency, the Department of Military Affairs is in charge of coordinating emergency activities.

MUTUAL AID AGREEMENTS: The Governor may enter into reciprocal aid agreements with other states or the neighboring provinces of foreign countries (such as British Columbia or, theoretically, Siberia). Alaska ratified the Interstate Civil Defense and Disaster Compact in 1977.

PUBLIC/PERSONAL LIABILITY: Volunteers and auxiliary civil defense workers reasonably attempting to comply with the Governor's orders are generally exempt from liability arising out of their activities. Persons who voluntarily allow the use of their property for shelter purposes are also immune.

LICENSING REQUIREMENTS: Licensing requirements may be suspended for skilled professionals licensed in other states.

CONTINUITY OF GOVERNMENT: The Governor may proclaim an emergency temporary location or locations for the seat of government inside or outside the state. The Governor is admonished to select locations which would not generally be considered military target sites. Alaska has no specific plan to deal with mass vacancies in state government in case of a catastrophe. The Governor is allowed to appoint successors to fill vacancies in the legislature and the executive and judicial branches of government.

Arizona

Title 26, Chapter 2, Sections 301 et seq.

DEFINITION:

An emergency is defined as the existence of conditions of disaster or of extreme peril to the safety of persons or property within the state, and includes air pollution, fire, flood, storm, epidemic, riot, or earthquake. A war emergency condition exists when the United States is attacked or the federal government warns the state that an attack is imminent.

DECLARATION
OF EMERGENCY:

The Governor is allowed to proclaim a state of war emergency or a state of emergency. The state of emergency is effective until terminated by the Governor or by concurrent resolution of the legislature. A state of war emergency terminates within 24 hours unless the Governor calls the legislature into session.

GOVERNOR'S
EMERGENCY POWERS:

During a state of war emergency, the Governor may suspend any statute, order, rule, or regulation that governs the conduct of state business if necessary, and may commandeer and utilize any property necessary during an emergency (property of the news media is not exempt from seizure). Reasonable compensation for the seizure of property is to be provided. During a state of emergency, the Governor has complete authority over all agencies of state government and may utilize all state personnel, equipment, and facilities as necessary to prevent or alleviate damage (but there is no authority granted for seizure of private property).

LEAD AGENCY:

The Division of Emergency Services, a component of the Arizona Department of Emergency and Military Affairs, is responsible for preparation for and response to emergencies and disasters. A State Emergency Council, consisting of the Governor, the Secretary of State, the Attorney General, and the Adjutant General, President of the Senate, and the Speaker of the House, and the directors of the Division of Emergency Services, the Department of Transportation, the Department of Health Services, and the Department of Public Safety, makes recommendations in the planning of emergencies. If the Governor is out of the state or otherwise inaccessible, the Director of Emergency Services may call a meeting of the Council and make a state of emergency proclamation, if at least three Council members (one of whom shall be an elected official) approve of the action.

MUTUAL AID
AGREEMENTS:

The Governor is allowed to enter into reciprocal aid agreements on behalf of the state. Arizona is a member of the Interstate Civil Defense and Disaster Compact.

PUBLIC/PERSONAL
LIABILITY:

Volunteers who are registered with the Division of Emergency Services, or unregistered persons placed into service during a state of war emergency and who comply with orders are immune from civil liability except for willful misconduct, gross negligence, or. bad faith.

LICENSING
REQUIREMENTS:

Professionals licensed under the laws of another state are permitted to operate without Arizona licenses in times of emergency.

CONTINUITY
OF GOVERNMENT:

Arizona has no provisions for emergency interim succession to state offices in case of a catastrophe, nor for moving the state capitol in an emergency. Legislative vacancies may be filled by election or by appointment by the county commissioners.

Arkansas

Title 11, Chapters 19 and 20

DEFINITION:

The Arkansas Emergency Services Act of 1973 defines a disaster as any tornado, storm, flood, high water, earthquake, drought, fire, radiological incident, air or surface-borne toxic or other hazardous material contamination, or other catastrophe, whether caused by natural forces, enemy attack or any other means, occurring anywhere in the state which the Governor thinks is, or will be, of sufficient severity and magnitude to warrant state action.

DECLARATION OF EMERGENCY:

The Governor may declare a disaster emergency if a disaster has occurred or is imminent. The state of emergency may continue for a maximum of 30 days unless renewed by the Governor, and may be terminated by the Governor or by the legislature at any time.

GOVERNOR'S EMERGENCY POWERS:

The Governor is commander-in-chief of all forces available for emergency duty. The Governor may suspend statutes, rules, and regulations prescribing the conduct of state business, if necessary; utilize all available governmental resources; direct evacuation; control entrance and exit to and from the disaster area; suspend the sale of alcohol, firearms, explosives, and combustibles; and commandeer or utilize any private property as necessary (with reasonable compensation, except for certain property such as standing timber). The Governor may maintain $1,000,000 fund for disaster relief.

LEAD AGENCY:

The Office of Emergency Services is charged with coordinating emergency relief and the prevention of disasters. The Director is appointed by the Governor, and the Office maintains a State Disaster Plan.

MUTUAL AID AGREEMENTS:

Arkansas enacted the Interstate Civil Defense and Disaster Compact in 1973. The Governor is not given authority to enter into other reciprocal agreements on behalf of the state.

PUBLIC/PERSONAL LIABILITY:

Article IV of the ICDDC allows licensed professionals from other states to practice in Arkansas during times of emergency. Persons who have voluntarily and without compensation granted the use of real estate, buildings, automotive vehicles, boats, and/or aircraft are immune from civil liability for death or injury caused to any person using such property. Qualified volunteer emergency service workers are also immune from civil liability, except for liability arising from willful misconduct or gross negligence.

CONTINUITY OF GOVERNMENT:

The Governor may move the seat of government if Little Rock is unsafe because of enemy attack. All executive officers and legislators are allowed to designate emergency interim successors to take their place in the event of a mass catastrophe. The Governor may appoint emergency judges to succeed members of the Supreme Court, and the Chief Justice may appoint successors to fill the lower courts.

California

§§ 8550 et seq. Title 2, Chapter 7

DEFINITION: California's Emergency Services Act defines three conditions of emergency. 1) a state of war emergency if the nation is attacked by an enemy, or when the federal government warns of an imminent attack; (2) air pollution or sudden and severe energy shortage, or plant or animal infestation or disease; (3) a local emergency, confined to a single county or city, but beyond local control.

DECLARATION OF EMERGENCY: A state of war emergency exists as soon as the United States is under enemy attack, without a Governor's proclamation. If a war emergency is likely to last longer than seven days, the Governor must convene the Emergency Council (described below) before the seventh day. The state of war emergency terminates if the Governor fails to convene the Emergency Council, or if the Governor fails to call the legislature into session within 30 days, or by proclamation of the Governor or the legislature that the emergency is at an end. A state of emergency may be declared by the Governor through a written proclamation filed with the Secretary of State. If the Governor is unavailable, the Director of the Office of Emergency Services may proclaim a state of emergency. The Governor is required to proclaim the termination of the state of emergency at the earliest possible date that conditions warrant. The state of emergency may be terminated by proclamation of the Governor or by concurrent resolution of the legislature. A local emergency may be proclaimed only by the governing body of a city or county and is not to last more than seven days unless ratified by the governing body.

GOVERNOR'S EMERGENCY POWERS: During an emergency, the Governor may suspend the provisions of any statute, order, rule, or regulation governing state business. The Governor may commandeer any private property or personnel as necessary, except for the news media, and may be granted complete authority over all agencies of the state government.

LEAD AGENCY: The Emergency Council is comprised of the Governor, the Lieutenant Governor, the Attorney General, and representatives of county governments, city governments, Red Cross, the fire services, and the law enforcement services. The President Pro Tempore of the Senate and the Speaker of the Assembly are required to participate on the Council, although all the elected members of the Council and the Attorney General may appoint alternates. The Emergency Council must develop a State Emergency Plan for the Governor's approval. The Office of Emergency Services is in charge of coordinating emergency activities during proclaimed emergencies.

MUTUAL AID AGREEMENTS: California joined the Interstate Civil Defense and Disaster Compact in 1951.

PUBLIC/PERSONAL LIABILITY: Volunteers registered with the Office of Emergency Services or the disaster council of any subdivision, and unregistered persons impressed into service during emergencies are immune from civil liability for torts that arise while performing their authorized duties. Physicians, surgeons, hospitals, nurses and dentists who render services during emergencies at the request of any state or local official are immune from liability, except in the case of willful acts and omissions. A public entity or emergency rescue personnel acting within the scope of employment are immune from liability for injuries caused by any action taken when providing emergency services unless the action was performed in bad faith or in a grossly negligent manner. The statute also establishes a presumption that the action was taken in good faith without gross negligence.

LICENSING REQUIREMENTS:	Professionals licensed in other states may render emergency assistance in California during an emergency without a license under Article IV of the ICDDC.
CONTINUITY OF GOVERNMENT:	California has a comprehensive statute dealing with succession to constitutional offices in the event of war or enemy-caused disaster. The Lieutenant Governor, Attorney General, Secretary of State, Treasurer and Controller shall each file with the Secretary of State the names of three to seven citizens qualified to be their respective successors, in order of preference. Each officer is required to appoint successors from different parts of the state to ensure the greatest probability of survival in the event of a disaster of some or all of the appointees. If none of the appointed successors survive, the office devolves upon one of the officer's deputies. If more than one-fifth of the membership of either house of the legislature becomes vacant, the remaining members, regardless of whether there is a quorum, may elect qualified successors to fill the empty seats. The Governor or Acting Governor may designate a new temporary state capitol in the event of any emergency.

Colorado

DEFINITION: The Colorado Disaster Emergency Act of 1973 defines a disaster as the occurrence or imminent threat of widespread or severe damage, injury, or loss of life or property resulting from any natural or man-made cause and includes oil spills, volcanic activity, and hostile military or paramilitary action.

DECLARATION OF EMERGENCY: The Governor may declare a disaster emergency by executive order or proclamation if a disaster has occurred or is threatened. The state of disaster emergency may be terminated at any time by gubernatorial proclamation or by joint resolution of the General Assembly, and may not continue for more than 30 days unless renewed by the Governor.

GOVERNOR'S EMERGENCY POWERS: The Governor is commander-in-chief of the organized and unorganized militia during a state of disaster emergency. The Governor may suspend all regulatory statutes and agency rules, orders, and regulations governing the conduct of state business, if necessary; utilize all available resources of the state government; direct evacuations; control movement within the disaster area; suspend the sale of alcohol, firearms, and explosives; and commandeer or utilize any private property necessary to cope with an emergency, with reasonable compensation to the owners (no exception for seizure of news media).

LEAD AGENCY: The Governor's Disaster Emergency Council, comprised of the Attorney General and the executive directors of the departments of administration, highways, local affairs, military affairs, and natural resources, and no more than three other members drawn from the directors of other executive departments, advises the Governor on all matters pertaining to the declaration of disasters. The Division of Disaster Emergency Services, which is part of the Department of Military Affairs, is responsible for the preparation and maintenance of the state disaster plan and for the coordination of emergency activities. The Division's director is advised by the Governor's Disaster Emergency Council. The director may establish rules governing expenditures from an established disaster emergency fund, and all expenditures from the fund are to be reviewed by the Council.

MUTUAL AID AGREEMENTS: The Governor is authorized to enter into interstate compacts for the prevention of disasters.

PUBLIC/PERSONAL LIABILITY: The owner of any building, mine, structure, or other real estate who makes that property available without compensation for civil defense is relieved from civil liability, except for willful or wanton acts that result in death or injury on the property.

LICENSING REQUIREMENTS: There is apparently no provision for the suspension of license requirements for skilled professionals during an emergency.

CONTINUITY OF GOVERNMENT: Colorado has no formal plan for filling vacancies in public offices after a catastrophe. The Constitution provides that the Governor or the Lieutenant Governor may transmit to the President of the Senate and Speaker of the House of Representatives a written declaration that s/he suffers from a physical or mental disability, and is unable to properly discharge the powers of the office. However, the Governor's physical or mental ability may also be determined by a majority of the Colorado Supreme Court after a hearing is held pursuant to a joint resolution adopted by two-thirds of all members of each house of the General Assembly. The Supreme Court on its own initiative then determines if and when such a disability exists. Such a determination is final and conclusive. Vacancies in the General Assembly may be filled by a vacancy committee that chooses qualified persons to fill empty seats and the Governor makes appointments to fill empty spaces in other state offices. There is no provision for emergency relocation of the seat of government.

Connecticut

Title 28, Chapters 517 and 518

DEFINITION:
Connecticut defines a civil preparedness emergency as an emergency declared by the Governor in the event of a serious natural disaster or of enemy attack, sabotage, or other hostile action within the state or a neighboring state, or the imminence of such an event.

DECLARATION
OF EMERGENCY:
The Governor may proclaim the existence of a state of civil preparedness emergency. The Governor is required to meet with the President Pro Tempore of the Senate, the Speaker of the House, and the majority and minority leaders of both houses on the advisability of calling a special session of the legislature. The legislature may also call itself into session during an emergency if a majority of the members of both houses so indicates. The state of emergency continues until the Governor declares it to be at an end, or a majority of the leaders of the General Assembly disapproves of the proclamation.

GOVERNOR'S
EMERGENCY POWERS:
The Governor is authorized to modify or suspend, in whole or in part any statute, regulation, or requirement, whenever, in his opinion, it is in conflict with the efficient and expeditious execution of civil preparedness functions during an emergency. Orders by the Governor have the full force and effect of law for six months, unless revoked sooner. The Governor may order all civil preparedness forces into action, order evacuations, and take possession of any land, buildings, equipment, horses, vehicles, aircraft, ships, food supplies, and fuel, if necessary (no exception for the news media). Property may be used by the Governor as s/he deems in the best interest of the State or its inhabitants, but compensation must be afforded.

LEAD AGENCY:
The Connecticut Office of Civil Preparedness is responsible for maintaining the Connecticut emergency operations plan and overseeing emergency activities during a state of civil preparedness emergency.

MUTUAL AID
AGREEMENTS:
Connecticut is a member of the Interstate Civil Defense and Disaster Compact.

PUBLIC/PERSONAL
LIABILITY:
Persons authorized to assist the civil preparedness forces during an emergency are immune from civil liability for the death of or injury to persons or for damage to property as a result of any such activity (exception for willful misconduct, but not for gross negligence). Persons who do not obey orders of civil preparedness forces may be subjected to a fine of up to $500. Persons who voluntarily allow their property to be used as shelter are exempt from civil liability.

LICENSING
REQUIREMENTS:
Requirements that skilled professionals be licensed before they can render aid may be suspended along with any other statute.

CONTINUITY
OF GOVERNMENT:
In case of emergency, the Governor may convene the General Assembly elsewhere, but the location must still be in Connecticut. There are no provisions for the filling of vacancies in state offices after a catastrophe (writs of election must be issued by Governor before legislative vacancies can be filled).

Delaware

Title 20, Chapter 31

DEFINITION: The Governor of Delaware is authorized to proclaim a state of emergency if s/he finds that a public disorder, disaster or emergency (not legally defined) exists within the state or any part thereof which affects life, health, property, or the public peace. Emergencies have included an acute shortage in usable energy resources and drought (as in 1978 and 1982 respectively).

DECLARATION OF EMERGENCY: The Governor may proclaim a state of emergency which continues indefinitely until the Governor declares it to be terminated.

GOVERNOR'S EMERGENCY POWERS: The Governor is allowed to impose restrictions on the possession and transportation of firearms and combustibles, the sale of alcoholic beverages and other commodities, and the presence of persons on public property, including streets and highways, as necessary. The Governor may promulgate orders, rules, and regulations that have the effect of law and that supersede all existing laws, ordinances, rules, and regulations that may conflict. The Governor is not specifically empowered to seize private property during an emergency.

LEAD AGENCY: The Division of Emergency Planning and Operations is part of the Department of Public Safety, and is in charge of creating and implementing Delaware's program for emergency planning and operations and the radiological emergency plan.

MUTUAL AID AGREEMENTS: Delaware has been a member of the Interstate Civil Defense and Disaster Compact since 1953.

PUBLIC/PERSONAL LIABILITY: Volunteer or auxiliary civilian defense workers are generally exempt from civil liability (except for willful or wanton misconduct) arising from their actions in emergencies. Persons who allow their property to be used for shelter are exempt from liability. Good samaritans acting in good faith to assist accident victims are exempted from liability generally at all times.

LICENSING REQUIREMENTS: The Governor may suspend licensing requirements by order and by authority of Article IV of the ICDDC.

CONTINUITY OF GOVERNMENT: The Constitution provides that the Governor may transmit to the President Pro Tempore of the Senate and the Speaker of the House of Representatives a written declaration that s/he is unable to discharge the powers and duties of the office. However, the Constitution also allows that the Chief Justice of the Delaware Supreme Court, the president of the Medical Society of Delaware, and the Commissioner of the Department of Mental Health, acting as a group, to submit to the President Pro Tempore and the Speaker their written declaration that the Governor is unable to carry out the powers and duties of the office because of mental or physical disability. Thereupon, if the General Assembly, within ten days of receipt of latter declaration, determines by two-thirds vote of all members elected to each house that the Governor is still unable, the Lieutenant Governor continues to discharge the duties of the office as Acting Governor. Delaware has a comprehensive plan for replacing all officers of the government after a catastrophe, contained in four statutes. Under the Emergency Interim Succession Acts, executive officers at all levels may designate three to seven qualified persons as successors who will serve until removed by the General Assembly. The Governor may designate emergency judges who will succeed to serve on all state courts until replaced. Legislators may designate qualified successors who are allowed to serve up to two years following an enemy attack. In the event of a threatened or actual enemy attack, the Governor may move the seat of government from Dover to any location or locations within or without Delaware for as long as necessary.

Florida

Chapter 252

DEFINITION:	The State Disaster Preparedness Act of 1974 defines a disaster as the occurrence or imminent threat of widespread or severe damage, injury, or loss of life or property resulting from any natural or manmade cause, including enemy attacks.
DECLARATION OF EMERGENCY:	The Governor may declare a state of disaster emergency, and may renew it if the emergency lasts more than 30 days. The Governor or the legislature may end a state of emergency at any time.
GOVERNOR'S EMERGENCY POWERS:	During an emergency, the Governor may suspend any law regulating the conduct of state business and any administrative laws, if necessary, and may commandeer or utilize property, subject to compensation to the owner. All gubernatorial orders shall have the force and effect of law and shall supersede any inconsistent laws. The orders of the Division of Public Safety Planning and Assistance are given similar weight. The Governor may not interfere with labor disputes or with the news media.
LEAD AGENCY:	The Division of Public Safety Planning and Assistance is part of the Department of Veteran and Community Affairs, and is responsible for preparing and implementing a comprehensive program to meet disasters and emergencies.
MUTUAL AID AGREEMENTS:	The Governor may enter into mutual aid agreements with other states. Florida has not enacted the Interstate Civil Defense and Disaster Compact into law.
PUBLIC/PERSONAL LIABILITY:	Persons who are property owners and voluntarily allow the use of their premises are generally immune from liability. Employees of the state (possibly including authorized volunteer workers) are immune from liability for torts arising out of their performance of duties.
CONTINUITY OF GOVERNMENT:	Florida provides for emergency succession for local officers, but not for legislators, judges, and state executive officers. In an emergency, the seat of government may be removed from Tallahassee to any other place or places. Vacancies in legislative offices can only be filled by special election.
	According to the Constitution, the Governor's inability to serve may be determined by the state Supreme Court after the docketing of a written "suggestion" by four cabinet members. The Constitution names the Secretary of State, Attorney General, Comptroller, Treasurer, Commissioner of Agriculture and Commissioner of Education as members of the Governor's cabinet in Florida. The Governor may also declare his physical inability to serve by filing a certificate with the Secretary of State. No specific mention is made of mental disability in the Constitution.

Georgia

DEFINITION: The Georgia Emergency Management Act of 1981 defines a disaster as any happening that causes great harm or damage, and an emergency as a sudden generally unexpected occurrence or set of circumstances demanding immediate action. The Governor is allowed to declare a state of emergency if s/he perceives that the threat or actual occurrence of a disaster or emergency is of sufficient severity and magnitude to warrant extraordinary assistance by the state to local authorities.

DECLARATION OF EMERGENCY: A state of emergency may be declared by the Governor and may be terminated either by the Governor or by concurrent resolution of the General Assembly. The emergency is not to last longer than 30 days unless the Governor renews it.

GOVERNOR'S EMERGENCY POWERS: During an emergency, the Governor may suspend all statutes that regulate the conduct of state business and the orders, rules, and regulations of any state agency, if necessary. The Governor may seize real property and commandeer or utilize any private property, as necessary, and may restrict movement, direct evacuation, and suspend the sale of alcohol, firearms, explosives, and combustibles. During an energy emergency, the Governor is not allowed to take possession of any property other than energy resources. There is no exception within the laws to prevent the seizure of the news media, and there appears to be no provision in the Emergency Management Act to compensate the owners of property that was seized or commandeered, and either lost or damaged.

LEAD AGENCY: The Emergency Management Division of the Georgia Department of Defense is responsible for preparing and carrying out the program for emergency management. The Director is authorized to make rules or regulations subject to the approval of the Governor.

MUTUAL AID AGREEMENTS: Georgia is a member of the Interstate Civil Defense and Disaster Compact.

PUBLIC/PERSONAL LIABILITY: Persons acting as volunteer emergency management workers are generally immune from civil liability arising from their activities. Persons who allow their property to be used as shelter for emergency purposes or who provide equipment for state use at no cost are immune from liability. Any person who acts in accordance with any emergency order, rule, or regulation promulgated by the Governor is made immune from civil liability under all circumstances.

LICENSING REQUIREMENTS: Article IV of the ICDDC allows for suspension of license requirements for professionals licensed in other states.

CONTINUITY OF GOVERNMENT: The Constitution provides that at the petition of any four constitutional elective officers, the state Supreme Court will determine the disability of the Governor by holding a public hearing. Not fewer than three physicians in private practice (at least one must be a psychiatrist) must testify during the hearing. The Court then rules on the mental or physical disability (temporary or permanent) of the Governor. If, after hearing the evidence on disability, the Supreme Court determines that there is a disability and that such a disability is permanent, the office is declared vacant and the successor to that office chosen as provided in the Constitution or under law. If the Court determines that the disability is temporary, it must also determine when the disability has ended and when the Governor may resume the exercise of the powers and duties of office. During the period of temporary disability, the powers of the office are exercised as provided by law. It is of particular note that this provision applies to all constitutional executive branch officers.

All state officers are also required to designate three to seven qualified persons as their emergency interim successors and to file a list with the Georgia Secretary of State within 30 days of taking office. If it becomes imprudent or impractical to have the seat of government in Atlanta, the Governor may designate an alternate location or locations to serve as the seat of government.

Hawaii

Title 10, Chapter 128

DEFINITION:
Hawaii's Civil Defense and Emergency Act gives the Governor certain powers to deal with enemy attacks, non-military manmade disasters, and natural disasters. The Governor may proclaim a Civil Defense Emergency Period if s/he believes that Hawaii has been or is in danger of being attacked by an enemy of the United States. The Governor may also proclaim an emergency period in order to minimize and repair injury and damage resulting from disasters caused by fire, flood, tidal wave, volcanic eruption, earthquake, or other natural disasters and major disasters caused by acts of man, including massive oil spills, nuclear accidents, airplane crashes, and civil disturbances.

DECLARATION
OF EMERGENCY:
The Governor may declare a period of emergency which lasts indefinitely until the Governor proclaims it terminated. This power may not be delegated.

GOVERNOR'S
EMERGENCY POWERS:
The Governor has the power to suspend any law which impedes the expeditious and efficient execution of civil defense and other emergency functions. The Governor may order quarantines, evacuations, blackouts, air raid drills, the suspension of water and gas services, and control of traffic as necessary. The Governor is specifically allowed to requisition and take possession of private property provided that notice is given to anyone on the premises and compensation is afforded. Orders of the Governor in an emergency have the force and effect of law.

LEAD AGENCY:
The Civil Defense Agency and the Disaster Relief Agency are divisions of the Governor's office in charge of preparing for emergencies and coordinating activity during periods of emergency. The Governor is also advised by the Civil Defense Advisory Council and the seven-member Disaster Relief Advisory Council, each appointed by the Governor.

MUTUAL AID
AGREEMENTS:
The Governor is allowed to enter into mutual aid agreements with other states on behalf of the State.

PUBLIC/PERSONAL
LIABILITY:
Volunteers whose services are accepted by an authorized civil defense official are exempted from tort liability during emergency, as a general rule. Persons and organizations who allow the use of their property for emergency purposes as shelter are likewise exempt. Hawaii also exempts all persons who render emergency care in good faith without expectation of remuneration under its Good Samaritan Law.

CONTINUITY
OF GOVERNMENT:
The Governor may move the seat of government to an emergency temporary location or locations in the case of an enemy attack, within or without the State. There is no emergency provision for filling vacancies in state offices after a catastrophe, but the Governor may appoint new legislators, judges, and executive officials if there are vacancies. New legislators must be of the same party as former legislators.

Idaho

Title 46, Chapter 10

DEFINITION:
The Idaho Disaster Preparedness Act of 1975 defines a disaster as the occurrence or imminent threat of widespread or severe damage, injury, loss of life, or property resulting from any natural or manmade cause.

DECLARATION OF EMERGENCY:
The Governor may declare a state of disaster emergency if a disaster has occurred or is imminent. The state of disaster emergency may be terminated at any time by the Governor or by both houses of the legislature, and may not continue for more than 30 days unless the Governor extends it for not more than another 30 days.

GOVERNOR'S EMERGENCY POWERS:
The Governor may suspend any regulations prescribing the conduct of public business if necessary; may issue orders having the effect of law that regulate conduct in the disaster area; and may commandeer or utilize any private property if necessary, subject to requirements for compensation of owners. The Governor may not interfere with a labor dispute, except to forestall imminent danger, and may not interfere with the dissemination of news and opinion.

LEAD AGENCY:
The Bureau of Disaster Services is part of the Military Division of the Office of the Governor, and is headed by the Adjutant General or by a chief appointed by the Adjutant General. The Bureau must prepare, maintain, and update a state disaster plan and coordinate all disaster activities.

MUTUAL AID AGREEMENTS:
The Governor may enter into interstate disaster compacts with any state.

PUBLIC/PERSONAL LIABILITY:
A person or entity owning any building or premises designated by the civil defense as a shelter will not generally be held civilly liable for most torts. No person under contract with the state to provide equipment or work to be used in disaster relief is subject to civil liability. There is no exemption provided for private persons who assist in disaster relief, although agents acting under a declaration by proper authority are immune from liability.

CONTINUITY OF GOVERNMENT:
Idaho has no plan to fill vacancies in the state government following a mass catastrophe. All vacancies in the executive, legislative, and judicial branches may be filled by appointees of the Governor. The legislature makes three nominations for each vacant legislative seat, and the Governor chooses one of the three nominees. Idaho has no provision for temporarily changing the seat of government in an emergency. Article X of the Idaho Constitution makes Boise the permanent site of the capital, and it can only be changed by popular vote. Sessions of the legislature may only be convened in Boise.

Illinois

DEFINITION: The Illinois Emergency Services and Disaster Agency Act of 1975 defines a disaster as an occurrence or threat of widespread or severe damage, injury, or loss of life or property resulting from any natural or manmade cause including oil spills, extended periods of severe weather, and critical shortages of essential fuels and energy.

DECLARATION OF EMERGENCY: The Governor may proclaim a disaster emergency for a period not to exceed 30 days (no provision for termination by the legislature).

GOVERNOR'S EMERGENCY POWERS: The Governor may suspend the provisions of any statute regulating the conduct of state business and the rules, regulations, and orders of any state agency, if necessary. The Governor may, on behalf of the state take possession of and acquire full title in such personal property as may be necessary to meet an emergency, including motor vehicles, aircraft, fuels, equipment, food, clothing, and medicine, as long as compensation is provided to the owners. The Governor may regulate movement of persons in the disaster area, and is given the power of prohibiting increases in the prices of goods and services during a disaster. The Governor may not interfere in a labor dispute, except when danger is threatened, nor may s/he interfere with the dissemination of news and opinions.

LEAD AGENCY: The State Emergency Services and Disaster Agency is responsible for developing programs of emergency services and disaster operations on all levels, and coordinating these programs during an emergency.

MUTUAL AID AGREEMENTS: The Governor may negotiate mutual aid agreements with other states and submit them for legislative approval. Illinois has been a member of the ICDDC since 1975.

PUBLIC/PERSONAL LIABILITY: Persons who voluntarily allow their property to be used for shelter in an emergency are exempt from civil liability. There is no formal immunity for volunteers assisting emergency service workers, although agents of the government are exempt from general civil liability.

CONTINUITY OF GOVERNMENT: Illinois has no provision for filling mass vacancies in the state government resulting from a catastrophe. The Constitution provides that the Governor may determine if s/he is impeded in the exercise of powers and, if so, may notify the Secretary of State and the next in line to the office, the Lieutenant Governor. The General Assembly by law may also specify by whom and what procedures the ability of the Governor to serve may be questioned. The state Supreme Court has original and exclusive jurisdiction to review the law and any determination of disability. In the absence of such a law, the Court may make the determination under such rules as it may adopt. Vacancies in executive and judicial offices are filled by gubernatorial appointment. Vacancies in the General Assembly are filled by appointment of the legislative committee of that legislative district of the political party of which the incumbent was a candidate at the time of his election. The Governor may move the seat of government in an emergency to any location or locations within or without the State of Illinois.

Indiana

DEFINITION: Indiana's Civil Defense Act of 1951 defines a disaster as occurrence or imminent threat of widespread or severe damage, injury, or loss of life or property resulting from any natural or manmade cause.

DECLARATION OF EMERGENCY: The Governor may proclaim a state of disaster emergency when a disaster has occurred or is threatened. The state of emergency may be terminated by either the Governor or by both houses of the General Assembly, but may not continue for more than 30 days unless renewed by the Governor.

GOVERNOR'S EMERGENCY POWERS: The Governor is commander-in-chief of the state militia and all emergency forces during a state of disaster emergency. The Governor may suspend the provisions of any statute regulating state business and any administrative laws if necessary; regulate the movement of persons within a disaster area; and commandeer or utilize any private property, if necessary, subject to reasonable compensation requirements. The Governor may not interfere with a labor dispute (unless absolutely necessary) or the dissemination of news.

LEAD AGENCY: The Governor is advised on matters of emergency by a State Civil Defense Advisory Council comprised of no more than 15 members appointed by the Governor from representatives of the State Chamber of Commerce, the Indiana Manufacturers Association, the State Federation of Labor, the Teamsters Union, the CIO, the Indiana Municipal League, the Indiana Farm Bureau, the Indiana Federation of Clubs, the American Legion, the VFW, the Indiana Congress of Parents and Teachers, the American Red Cross, the Indiana State Medical Association, the Hoosier State Press Association, the Indiana Society for Public Administration, and the Indiana State Board of Realtors. Members of the Council are paid for their reasonable expenses, and are required to meet quarterly to recommend changes in the state disaster plan. The Department of Civil Defense is in charge of preparing, maintaining, and implementing the state disaster plan, and coordinating all emergency activities.

MUTUAL AID AGREEMENTS: Indiana has been a member of the Interstate Civil Defense and Disaster Compact since 1953.

PUBLIC/PERSONAL LIABILITY: Persons who allow the state to use their buildings and real property for civil defense purposes are generally granted immunity from tort liability. Volunteers who are accepted as civil defense and disaster workers are also generally granted immunity for all actions performed in compliance with the Governor's orders during an emergency.

LICENSING REQUIREMENTS: The Governor may suspend license requirements for skilled professionals licensed in other states during a state of disaster emergency.

CONTINUITY OF GOVERNMENT: Indiana has no provision for filling mass vacancies in state offices after a catastrophe. The Constitution provides that the Governor may transmit to the President Pro Tempore of the Senate and Speaker of the House of Representatives a written declaration that s/he is unable to discharge the powers and duties of the office. However, the President Pro Tempore and the Speaker may also file with the Indiana Supreme Court a written statement suggesting that the Governor is unable to serve. The Court must then meet within 48 hours to decide the question of the Governor's disability. Executive and judicial offices are filled by gubernatorial appointment, and legislative vacancies are filled by party precinct committeemen. The Governor may move the seat of government to any other location or locations during an enemy attack, if necessary.

Iowa

DEFINITION: Iowa law provides for two types of crises during which the Governor may proclaim a state of emergency. A public disorder emergency arises when there is substantial enough interference with the public peace to constitute a significant threat to property, health, and safety of the people. A disaster emergency includes manmade and natural catastrophes that threaten public peace, health, safety, or which damage public and private property.

DECLARATION OF EMERGENCY: The Governor may proclaim the existence of either type of emergency, and either the Governor or the General Assembly may terminate the emergency. If the General Assembly is out of session, the emergency may be terminated by a majority vote of the Legislative Council (composed of 20 members, including all the officers of the legislature). Public disorder emergencies may not continue longer than ten days, and disaster emergencies are limited to 30 days.

GOVERNOR'S EMERGENCY POWERS: During a public disorder emergency, the Governor may order curfews; limit public gatherings; curtail the sale and possession of articles such as explosives, firearms, combustibles, and alcoholic beverages; and limit the use of streets and highways. During a state of disaster emergency, the Governor may suspend the provisions of statutes regulating the conduct of state business and any state administrative laws; regulate the movement of persons within the disaster area; and commandeer and utilize any private property as necessary, subject to requirements for compensation.

LEAD AGENCY: The Office of Disaster Services is a division of the Department of Public Defense. It is responsible for the administration of emergency planning, and must prepare and coordinate any disaster or public disorder emergency plans.

MUTUAL AID AGREEMENTS: The Governor may enter into agreements with other states. Iowa is a member of the Interstate Civil Defense and Disaster Compact.

PUBLIC/PERSONAL LIABILITY: Iowa is one of the few states that has no provision within its civil defense act to exempt the state agencies and their workers from civil liability arising out of an emergency. Iowa does, however, have a Good Samaritan Law that exempts any person who in good faith renders emergency care or assistance without compensation from civil liability as a general matter.

LICENSING REQUIREMENTS: During a state of disaster emergency, the Governor may suspend license requirements for skilled professionals.

CONTINUITY OF GOVERNMENT Iowa has no law to govern the filling of mass vacancies in state government following a catastrophe. Either the person next in line of succession to the office of Governor or the Chief Justice of the state Supreme Court may convene a conference to determine if the Governor is unable to discharge the duties of office. Conference members include the Chief Justice, the Director of Mental Health, and the Dean of Medicine at the State University of Iowa. By secret ballot and unanimous vote, the conference members may find the Governor temporarily unable to fulfill the duties of office. If either the Director of Mental Health or the Dean of Medicine is not a physician, that person may appoint a staff member to convene a conference. Whenever the Governor believes that the disability has been removed, s/he may convene the conference. The three members must, within ten days, examine the Governor and, within seven days, conduct a secret ballot to find if the disability is removed. Executive and judicial offices are filled by gubernatorial appointment, and legislative seats are filled by special election. Iowa Code § 2.1 implies that the Governor may convene the state legislature at some other place in times of pestilence or public danger, but there is no provision specifically giving the Governor the power to change the seat of government.

Kansas

DEFINITION: The Kansas Emergency Preparedness Act defines a disaster as the occurrence or threat of widespread or severe damage, injury, or loss of life or property resulting from any natural or manmade cause.

DECLARATION OF EMERGENCY: The Governor may proclaim a state of disaster emergency, or, if s/he is absent, the Lieutenant Governor may do so. A state of disaster emergency may be terminated by the Governor or by both houses of the legislature. No state of emergency may continue for more than 15 days unless ratified by the Legislature, however, the State Finance Council (comprised of nine members drawn from the leadership of the legislature) may extend the state of emergency by 30 days by majority vote if the Governor so requests.

GOVERNOR'S EMERGENCY POWERS: The Governor may suspend statutes regulatory of the state business and any administrative laws; may regulate conduct within the disaster area; may commandeer and utilize private property, if necessary, with compensation to the owners. The Governor is not allowed to interfere with labor disputes, unless public safety is threatened, nor with the dissemination of news. The Lieutenant Governor is allowed to exercise the Governor's emergency powers if the Governor is out of state.

LEAD AGENCY: The Division of Emergency Preparedness is part of the state Office of Adjutant General and is in charge of preparing, maintaining, and implementing a state disaster emergency plan and a state resources management plan to deal with emergencies.

MUTUAL AID AGREEMENTS: Kansas is a member of the Interstate Civil Defense and Disaster Compact.

PUBLIC/PERSONAL LIABILITY: Volunteer workers assisting in emergency activities are generally immune from civil liability. Persons who voluntarily allow their property to be used as shelter in connection with civil defense are also afforded general immunity.

LICENSING REQUIREMENTS: The Governor may suspend license requirements for skilled professionals licensed in other states under a state of disaster emergency.

CONTINUITY OF GOVERNMENT: Under the Emergency Interim Executive and Judicial Succession Act, the Governor or Acting Governor designates emergency interim successors for all state officers and for the Supreme Court justices when vacancies arise in an emergency. The Chief Justice, in consultation with the other justices, establishes successors for all the lower courts. Under the Emergency Interim Legislative Succession Act, the district committees of state political party organizations appoint qualified persons to fill vacant seats in the legislature in an emergency, along party lines. If the Governor, Lieutenant Governor, President of the Senate, and the Speaker of the House are all incapacitated or killed in a catastrophe, the Governor's office is filled in the following order: Secretary of State; Attorney General; Chancellor of Kansas University; and, President of Kansas State University. The Governor is allowed to transfer the seat of government during an emergency to any location or locations within the State of Kansas.

Kentucky

DEFINITION: Kentucky defines a disaster as any incident or situation so declared by executive order of the Governor and includes natural and man-caused disasters, including energy shortages and transportation emergencies, or the threat of same.

DECLARATION
OF EMERGENCY: The Governor may declare a state of emergency for an indefinite period of time. Kentucky has no provision for the termination of a state of emergency.

GOVERNOR'S
EMERGENCY POWERS: The Governor may issue orders, rules, and regulations that have the force and effect of law, and that effectively suspend any inconsistent existing laws. The Governor may regulate conduct within the disaster area as s/he feels is necessary, and s/he may seize property for the protection of the public or at the request of the President of the United States, with reasonable compensation to property owners. No limitations are placed on the Governor's powers to seize property.

LEAD AGENCY: The Division of Disaster and Emergency Services is a part of the Department of Military Affairs (also called the Emergency Management Agency) and is headed by the Adjutant General of the Commonwealth of Kentucky. The Division, acting under the authority of the Adjutant General, is empowered to prepare, maintain, and implement a comprehensive disaster plan for the state. The Adjutant General may issue orders, rules, and regulations that have substantially the same force as those issued by the Governor under a state of emergency.

MUTUAL AID
AGREEMENTS: The Adjutant General is allowed to enter into reciprocal aid agreements pursuant to executive order or legislative act. Kentucky is a member of the Interstate Civil Defense and Disaster Compact.

PUBLIC/PERSONAL
LIABILITY: Volunteer emergency workers who are reasonably attempting to comply with orders issued in an emergency are generally exempted from civil liability. Persons owning property who voluntarily allow it to be used as shelter for emergency purposes are also generally exempted from civil liability.

LICENSING
REQUIREMENTS: During a state of emergency, the Governor may suspend license requirements for skilled professionals.

CONTINUITY
OF GOVERNMENT: Kentucky has no provision for filling mass vacancies in state government following a catastrophe. Vacant seats in the General Assembly must be filled by special election, and vacancies in state offices are filled by election or appointment. In case of war, insurrection, or pestilence, the Governor may order the legislature to assemble in a location other than Frankfort.

Louisiana

DEFINITION: Louisiana does not define the criteria for declaration of a state of
                       emergency, but does concern itself with the possibility of the occurrences
                       of disasters of unprecedented size and destructiveness resulting from
                       hostile action, or from natural causes.

DECLARATION   The Governor is allowed to declare a state of emergency, and state of
OF EMERGENCY: emergency may last indefinitely.

GOVERNOR'S   The Governor is not granted specific powers but is authorized to make,
EMERGENCY POWERS: amend, and rescind the necessary orders, rules, and regulations to protect
                       public safety. No provision of the Act gives the Governor's orders the
                       effect of, or superiority over, existing laws, but violation of an order
                       promulgated during an emergency is a misdemeanor punishable by up to a $500
                       fine and/or up to six months in the parish jail.

LEAD AGENCY: The Louisiana Department of Public Safety has taken over all the functions
                       of the old Civil Defense Agency (abolished 1977), which was in charge of
                       preparing, maintaining, and implementing a state program for civil defense.

MUTUAL AID   The Adjutant General is authorized to enter into reciprocal civil defense
AGREEMENTS: aid and assistance agreements on behalf of the State.

PUBLIC/PERSONAL   Louisiana has no provision to exempt volunteers aiding in emergency
LIABILITY: activities from liability. Louisiana also does not provide immunity to
                       persons who voluntarily allow their property to be used as shelter in an
                       emergency.

LICENSING   The Governor has no specific power to waive license requirements.
REQUIREMENTS:

CONTINUITY   Louisiana has three Emergency Interim Succession Acts to fill vacancies in
OF GOVERNMENT: state offices after a mass catastrophe. The Louisiana Constitution has
                       general provisions for the declaration and/or determination of the
                       inability of any statewide elective official to serve. The official may
                       transmit a written declaration to the presiding officers of the Senate and
                       the House. However, the ability of the Governor to serve may also be
                       called into question when a majority of the statewide elected officials
                       (including the Lieutenant Governor) transmit a written declaration to the
                       presiding officer of each house and to the Governor, and file a copy with
                       the Secretary of State. The Lieutenant Governor assumes office as Acting
                       Governor unless, within 48 hours after the declaration is filed with the
                       Secretary of State's office, the Governor files a counter-declaration. In
                       that case, the state legislature convenes on the third calendar day after
                       the counter-filing. If two-thirds of the elected membership of each house
                       fails to adopt a resolution within 72 hours declaring probable
                       justification for the determination that inability exists, the Governor
                       remains in office. Otherwise, the Lieutenant Governor assumes the powers
                       and duties of the office. The Constitution also provides that the state
                       Supreme Court may, by a majority vote of members elected to the Court,
                       determine the issue of inability after due notice and hearing. However, a
                       judgment of the Court affirming inability may be reconsidered, either upon
                       its own motion or upon the application of the Governor. Upon proper
                       showing, and by a majority vote of its elected members, the Court may
                       determine that no inability exists.

                       Executive officers and legislators may also designate three to seven
                       qualified persons to succeed them. The Governor designates successors for
                       the Supreme Court, and the Chief Justice chooses successors for the
                       inferior courts. The Governor may change the seat of government to another
                       location or locations if necessary.

Maine

Title 37A, Chapter 3

DEFINITION: The Maine Civil Emergency Preparedness Act defines a disaster as the occurrence or imminent threat of widespread or severe damage, injury, or loss of life or property resulting from any natural or manmade cause. An energy emergency is an actual or impending acute shortage in usable energy resources.

DECLARATION OF EMERGENCY: The Governor may proclaim that an emergency exists, or, if the Governor is absent from the State, the person next in line of succession may proclaim an emergency. The emergency continues indefinitely until the Governor is satisfied that an emergency no longer exists.

GOVERNOR'S EMERGENCY POWERS: The Governor is allowed to make necessary orders, rules, and regulations that suspend the operation of any inconsistent laws during the emergency. The Governor may also exercise power of eminent domain over all private property necessary to be used during an emergency, with compensation. During an energy emergency, the Governor may not exercise eminent domain powers but may limit the sale and use of energy resources. The Governor must convene the legislature if the energy emergency is to be in effect for more than 90 days. During all emergencies, the Governor has the power to enlist the aid of any person to assist in disaster activities. Failure to comply with such an order is a Class E crime punishable by a fine of up to $1000 and/or 11 months in prison.

LEAD AGENCY: A Civil Defense Preparedness Council, comprised of five members appointed by the Governor, advises the Governor and the director of the Bureau of Civil Emergency Preparedness on emergency matters. The Bureau is part of the office of the Adjutant General and is in charge of preparing and implementing a program for state emergencies.

MUTUAL AID AGREEMENTS: The Governor may enter into mutual aid arrangements with other states and foreign countries. Maine is a member of the Interstate Civil Defense and Disaster Compact.

PUBLIC/PERSONAL LIABILITY: Persons who voluntarily permit the use of their premises for emergency preparedness activities are exempt from liability. Persons ordered to assist in disaster activities are also apparently generally immune from civil liability.

LICENSING REQUIREMENTS: The Governor may suspend license requirements for skilled professionals licensed in other states during an emergency.

CONTINUITY OF GOVERNMENT: Maine has no plan for filling mass vacancies in the state government following a catastrophe. Maine formerly had several Emergency Interim Succession Acts but repealed them in 1977. Legislative vacancies are to be filled by special election, and other vacancies are filled by gubernatorial appointment. The Governor may establish an emergency temporary location or locations for the seat of government, if necessary.

Maryland

Article 16A

DEFINITION:	The State Emergency Management and Civil Defense Act defines an emergency as the threat or occurrence of enemy attack or any hurricane, tornado, other disaster, or other catastrophe which requires state emergency assistance in order to save lives and protect public health and safety.
DECLARATION OF EMERGENCY:	The Governor may declare a state of emergency, and it may be terminated at any time by either the Governor or by the legislature. In any event, no state of emergency can last more than 30 days unless renewed by the Governor.
GOVERNOR'S EMERGENCY POWERS:	The Governor may suspend the provisions of any statute, rule, or regulation if necessary. The Governor may authorize the utilization of any private property if the owners are compensated for damage or loss, and may regulate private conduct in the disaster area.
LEAD AGENCY:	The Emergency Management Advisory Council is composed of members of local governments and organizations of firefighters and rescue workers, selected by the Governor for advice in times of emergency. Council members are not paid, but may be reimbursed for their expenses. The State Emergency Management and Civil Defense Agency is a division of the Department of Public Safety and Corrections, and is responsible for preparing and implementing the state emergency management program.
MUTUAL AID AGREEMENTS:	The Governor may cooperate with other states on matters pertaining to emergency management. Maryland is a member of the Interstate Emergency Management and Civil Defense Compact (Interstate Civil Defense and Disaster Compact).
PUBLIC/PERSONAL LIABILITY:	Maryland exempts the employees of emergency management groups from liability for their actions, but makes no provision for volunteer workers not formally employed. Maryland does not exempt persons who allow their property to be used as shelter from liability.
LICENSING REQUIREMENTS:	The Governor may suspend license requirements for skilled professionals licensed in other states during a state of emergency.
CONTINUITY OF GOVERNMENT:	The Constitution provides that the Governor may notify the Lieutenant Governor in writing of the fact that s/he is temporarily unable to perform the duties of the office. However, when the Governor is unable to communicate his or her inability, the General Assembly, by an affirmative vote of three-fifths of all members in joint session, may adopt a resolution declaring the Governor or Lieutenant Governor to be unable, by reason of physical or mental disability, to perform the duties of office. The officer who concludes that the Governor is unable to perform has the power to call the General Assembly into joint session. The resolution of the General Assembly is then delivered to the state Court of Appeals. The Court has exclusive jurisdiction to determine whether the Governor is unable to perform the duties of office, and may, in accordance with its decision, declare the office to be vacant. If the disability is deemed to be temporary, the Court has continuing jurisdiction to determine when the disability ends. Maryland has no provision for filling mass vacancies in state offices arising from a catastrophe, although if the mayor or chief official in any town is killed, the County Council may appoint a temporary replacement; if the Mayor of Baltimore, or a majority of the Board of County Commissioners, County Council or City Council are killed, the Governor may assume control of the government of Baltimore. The General Assembly may replace elected or appointed officials who become incapacitated, are missing, or are dead. Annapolis is the permanent seat of government, and the legislature is not to be convened or held at any other place except if absolutely necessary.

Massachusetts

DEFINITION: The Civil Defense Act allows the Governor to declare a state of emergency upon the occurrence of any disaster or catastrophe resulting from hostile action or natural causes. Emergencies include the accidental release of radiation from a nuclear power plant.

DECLARATION OF EMERGENCY: The Governor is allowed to declare a state of emergency for an indefinite period of time. Massachusetts makes no provisions for terminating a state of emergency.

GOVERNOR'S EMERGENCY POWERS: The Governor may take possession of any land, buildings, machinery, equipment, horses, motor vehicles, aircraft, boats, food, or fuel supplies if necessary, but compensation must be afforded to owners. The Governor may also issue executive orders that supersede any existing laws if necessary. Violation of an order promulgated by the Governor is punishable by up to a year in prison and/or a fine of $500.

LEAD AGENCY: The Civil Defense Agency and Office of Emergency Preparedness are in charge of preparing and carrying out the program for civil defense of the Commonwealth. The Civil Defense Advisory Council is appointed by the Governor from among department heads and officers of the Commonwealth, who advise the Governor on matters pertaining to emergencies.

MUTUAL AID AGREEMENTS: The Governor is allowed to cooperate with other states in all matters pertaining to civil defense.

PUBLIC/PERSONAL LIABILITY: Persons who are engaged in civil defense activities and who are in good faith attempting to comply with the Governor's orders, are generally exempt from civil liability. Persons who voluntarily allow the use of their property as shelter are similarly exempt.

CONTINUITY OF GOVERNMENT: The Constitution provides that the Governor's office becomes vacant when the Governor transmits to the President of the Senate and House Speaker a written declaration that s/he is unable to discharge the powers and duties of office. However, the Chief Justice and majority of the associate justices of the state Supreme Court (or other body designated by the state legislature) may also transmit to the President and Speaker a letter suggesting that the Governor is unable to discharge the powers and duties of the office. Thereafter, whenever the Governor transmits to the President and Speaker a written declaration that no disability exists, the vacancy is deemed terminated after four days, unless the Chief Justice and majority of the associate justices (or other body) transmit within four days their declaration that the Governor is unable to discharge the powers and duties of the office. In that case, the General Court (the state legislature) decides the question of the Governor's disability, assemblying within 48 hours if not already in session. If the General Court, within 21 days of receipt of the justices' declaration, determines that the Governor is unable to discharge the powers of the office, the office remains vacant. This constitutional provision is also applicable to the Lieutenant Governor when the Lieutenant Governor is performing the duties of the Governor's office.

During an emergency, the Governor may appoint successors to appointed state offices without the approval of the General Court (the legislature). Commissioners and the heads of executive and administrative departments must designate five possible successors within their departments. There is no provision for mass vacancies in the legislature or in the courts, nor is there a provision for moving the seat of government in times of emergency.

Michigan

Chapter 30

DEFINITION: Michigan's Emergency Preparedness Act defines a disaster as the occurrence or threat of widespread or severe damage, injury, or loss of life or property resulting from a natural or manmade causes, and includes hazardous peacetime radiological incidents and major transportation accidents. Riots and civil disorders are not within the meaning of disasters.

DECLARATION OF EMERGENCY: The Governor may declare a state of disaster to last not more than 14 days unless s/he requests an extension for a specific number of days that is approved by the legislature.

GOVERNOR'S EMERGENCY POWERS: The Governor may suspend statutes, orders, and rules that regulate the conduct of state business if necessary. Criminal process and procedures, however, may not be suspended. The Governor may also commandeer or utilize private property if necessary, subject to compensation of the owner. Violation of orders issued by the Governor is a misdemeanor.

LEAD AGENCY: The Department of State Police is in charge of preparing, maintaining, and implementing the Michigan emergency preparedness plan. If other departments and agencies of state government are required by the plan to provide an annex to the plan, they are to employ an emergency services coordinator to serve as a liaison between his or her department and the Department of State Police. A 15-member Emergency Preparedness Advisory Council advises the Governor.

MUTUAL AID AGREEMENTS: The Governor is allowed to enter into reciprocal aid agreements with any other state, and any neighboring province of Canada. Michigan is a member of the Interstate Disaster Compact (Interstate Civil Defense and Disaster Compact).

PUBLIC/PERSONAL LIABILITY: Volunteer and auxiliary disaster relief workers reasonably attempting to comply with orders by the Governor are immune from civil liability. Persons licensed to practice medical services anywhere in the United States, who are rendering services at the request of disaster officials, are not liable for an injury sustained by a person by reason of those services, regardless of how or under what circumstances or by what cause those injuries are sustained, except in the case of willful acts or omissions. Persons who own property and voluntarily allow it to be used as shelter are generally immune from liability, but they are legally obligated to make known the existence of hidden dangers on the premises.

LICENSING REQUIREMENTS: The Governor may suspend license requirements for skilled professionals licensed in other states during a state of disaster.

CONTINUITY OF GOVERNMENT: The Constitution provides that the inability of the Governor be determined by a majority of the state Supreme Court upon joint request of the President Pro Tempore of the Senate and the Speaker of the House of Representatives. The court, on its own initiative, determines when the inability ceases. The Governor must designate five emergency interim successors, scattered throughout the state, to supplement his or her constitutional successors. All other executive officers must also designate five successors each. The legislative and judicial branches do not have statutory emergency interim succession procedures. All persons designated as successors are legally obligated to stay informed of the duties of the office to which they have been designated. The legislature may be called into session by any two of its leaders after a disaster, and may meet elsewhere if Lansing is neither convenient nor safe enough to serve as a seat of government.

Minnesota

Chapter 12

DEFINITION:
The Minnesota Civil Defense Act of 1951 allows the Governor to declare a civil defense emergency if the United States is attacked or after the occurrence of a major disaster from enemy sabotage or other hostile action. The Governor may declare a peacetime emergency when an act of nature, industrial accident, or hazardous materials accident endangers life and property, and local government resources are inadequate to handle the situation.

DECLARATION OF EMERGENCY:
The Governor may declare a civil defense emergency that lasts up to 30 days if the legislature is in session or if s/he immediately calls both houses into session. A peacetime emergency may only last for five days, unless extended for up to 30 days by a resolution of the Executive Council (which consists of the Governor, Lieutenant Governor, Secretary of State, State Auditor, State Treasurer, and Attorney General). The Governor may terminate emergencies at any time.

GOVERNOR'S EMERGENCY POWERS:
In an emergency, the Governor has the power to issue orders that have the effect of law, and supersede any conflicting laws for the duration of the emergency. However, all orders must be approved by the Executive Council before they can take effect. The Governor, and persons that s/he designates within state and local civil defense organizations to give orders, are allowed to order any private citizen to perform services for civil defense purposes, and may commandeer any personal property for use in an emergency, subject to compensation requirements.

LEAD AGENCY:
The Division of Emergency Services is part of the Department of Public Safety, and is in charge of preparing and implementing a comprehensive program for emergency management to be used in times of crisis. The Division also is in charge of developing a nuclear power plant emergency response plan for each nuclear power plant located in Minnesota.

MUTUAL AID AGREEMENTS:
The Governor may enter into mutual aid arrangements with other states. Minnesota is a member of the Civilian Defense Compact.

PUBLIC/PERSONAL LIABILITY:
Minnesota has no provision to shield persons who render aid in an emergency from civil liability. However, any person ordered to perform services in an emergency must perform those services or be found guilty of a misdemeanor, and can be imprisoned for up to 90 days.

LICENSING REQUIREMENTS:
Persons licensed in other states are not required to be licensed in Minnesota before they can render aid in an emergency.

CONTINUITY OF GOVERNMENT:
The legislature may provide for continuity of government in periods of emergency resulting from disasters caused by enemy attack. Thus far, it has not done so. The Governor may relocate the seat of government from St. Paul to any other location if necessary.

Mississippi

Title 33, Chapter 15

DEFINITION:

The Mississippi Emergency Management Law allows the Governor to declare two types of emergencies. A state of war emergency arises from the threat or occurrence of an attack on the United States. A state of emergency means that conditions of disaster or extreme peril to the safety of persons or property within the state, caused by natural or manmade conditions, have occurred or are threatened.

DECLARATION
OF EMERGENCY:

A state of war emergency can take effect immediately, without gubernatorial proclamation, when the United States is attacked or the federal government warns that such attack is imminent. The Governor or the legislature may terminate the state of war emergency by proclamation or concurrent resolution. A state of emergency may also be proclaimed by the Governor if s/he finds that a disaster is beyond local control. A state of emergency may last indefinitely, but the Governor is advised to terminate it at the earliest possible date that conditions warrant.

GOVERNOR'S
EMERGENCY POWERS:

The Governor may suspend the provisions of any statute regulating the conduct of state business and any administrative laws if necessary. S/he may also commandeer or utilize any private property as necessary, provided that the owners are compensated. These powers apply during both types of states of emergency. The Governor's orders have the effect of law and supersede existing laws.

LEAD AGENCY:

The Mississippi Emergency Management Council is appointed by the Governor for advice on emergency matters. The Mississippi Emergency Management Agency is in charge of preparing and implementing a state program for emergency management during times of crisis.

MUTUAL AID
AGREEMENTS:

The Governor is authorized to enter into mutual aid agreements with other states and neighboring provinces of foreign countries. Mississippi is a member of the Interstate Civil Defense and Disaster Compact.

PUBLIC/PERSONAL
LIABILITY:

Persons who own property and voluntarily allow it to be used as shelter for emergency purposes are generally exempt from liability. Volunteer emergency workers are not specifically granted immunity, but agents of the government are granted immunity during an emergency.

CONTINUITY
OF GOVERNMENT:

The Governor may convene the state legislature at the seat of government, or at a different place if Jackson has become dangerous because of enemy attack or from disease. Mississippi has no provision for filling mass vacancies in state offices following a catastrophe. Legislative vacancies shall be filled by special election, and other vacancies by gubernatorial appointment.

Should a doubt arise as to whether a vacancy has occurred in the office of the Governor or as to whether any of the disabilities shall have ended, the Constitution provides that the Secretary of State may submit the question to the judges of the state Supreme Court. A majority of the Court investigates the question and furnishes the Secretary a written opinion. The Court's opinion is final and conclusive.

Missouri

Chapter 44

DEFINITION:

Missouri law allows an emergency to be declared when an attack upon the United States is anticipated or has occurred, or upon the actual occurrence of a natural diaster of major proportions. Manmade disasters are apparently not covered by the act, nor is the threat of a natural disaster.

DECLARATION
OF EMERGENCY:

The Governor or the legislature may declare the existence of an emergency, and either may terminate it. An emergency may technically last indefinitely, since there is no time limitation upon the duration of a declaration of emergency.

GOVERNOR'S
EMERGENCY POWERS:

During an emergency, the Governor may seize any means of transportation, other than railroads; any radio, telephone, or telegraph system (no exception for news media); necessary buildings for housing and hospitalization; and all stocks of fuel. The Governor may also regulate the distribution, shipment, and prices of necessary goods.

LEAD AGENCY:

The Disaster Planning and Operations Office, Civil Defense, is part of the Office of the Adjutant General and is in charge of implementing the state program for civil defense. A State Emergency Resources Planning Committee, drawn from volunteers representative of industry, commerce, labor, agriculture, governmental, and professional groups, is in charge of formulating a comprehensive plan for management of resources in time of emergency.

MUTUAL AID
AGREEMENTS:

The Governor is authorized to enter into reciprocal agreements with other states.

PUBLIC/PERSONAL
LIABILITY:

Missouri's civil defense laws do not specifically exempt anyone from civil liability in an emergency. Missouri is one of the few states that does not immunize property owners who allow their premises to be used as shelter from liability. However, an opinion of the Attorney General of November 14, 1953 states that volunteer participants in the civil defense program who exercise due care in following lawful orders issued under the Civil Defense Law are immune from liability.

LICENSING
REQUIREMENTS:

The Governor may waive any statutory requirement regarding licensing or certification of skills. This differs from the usual waiver of licenses that applies only to persons licensed in another state--it applies to any license requirement.

CONTINUITY
OF GOVERNMENT:

Missouri has no provision for filling mass vacancies in state offices in an emergency. Vacancies in the legislature must be filled by election. The seat of government is fixed in Jefferson City, and neither house shall, without the consent of the other, adjourn to any other place than that in which the two houses are sitting.

The Governor may transmit to the President Pro Tempore of the Senate and the Speaker of the House of Representatives his written declaration of disability. However, the Constitution also provides that a majority of the Disability Board (comprised of the Lieutenant Governor, Secretary of State, State Auditor, State Treasurer, Attorney General, President Pro Tempore of the Senate, Speaker of the House, the Majority Floor Leader of the Senate, and the Majority Floor Leader of the House) may transmit to the President Pro Tempore and the Speaker their written declaration that the Governor is unable to discharge the powers and duties of the office.

Montana

Title 10, Chapter 3

DEFINITION: Montana law covers several types of emergency conditions. A state of emergency may be declared when there is an imminent threat of disaster causing immediate peril to life or property. A state of disaster may be declared after the actual occurrence of a disaster (defined as the occurrence of widespread or severe damage, injury, or loss of life or property, resulting from any natural or manmade cause). A post-attack recovery and rehabilitation emergency may be proclaimed following an enemy attack.

DECLARATION OF EMERGENCY: All three types of emergencies may be proclaimed by the Governor. A state of emergency is to last only 20 days, unless the legislature extends it, or the President of the United States declares an emergency. A state of disaster is to last only 30 days, unless renewed by the legislature or the President. The legislature may terminate either type of emergency at any time, as may the Governor. A state of post-attack recovery and rehabilitation emergency will terminate automatically after six months. If it is proclaimed, the Governor must call the legislature into session within 45 days. The post-attack emergency may be terminated at any time.

GOVERNOR'S EMERGENCY POWERS: During non-military emergencies, the Governor serves as commander-in-chief of the state militia and all emergency forces, and may suspend statutes regulating the conduct of state business and administrative laws if necessary. The Governor is not given the authority to seize property. During a post-attack emergency, the Governor may issue orders, rules, and regulations that have the effect of law and supersede inconsistent laws. The Governor may make all necessary orders to preserve resources after an enemy attack.

LEAD AGENCY: The Division of Disaster and Emergency Services is part of the Department of Military Affairs. The Division is in charge of preparing, maintaining, and carrying out the state disaster and emergency plan and program.

MUTUAL AID AGREEMENTS: The Governor is permitted to enter into the Interstate Civil Defense and Disaster Compact, and Montana joined the Compact in 1951.

PUBLIC/PERSONAL LIABILITY: Volunteer and auxiliary civil defense workers are generally immune from liability for their actions during a non-military emergency. There is no corresponding provision for post-attack emergencies. Montana also has no provision for persons who allow property to be used for shelter purposes.

LICENSING REQUIREMENTS: Under the Interstate Civil Defense and Disaster Compact, the Governor may suspend licensing requirements for skilled professionals licensed in other states.

CONTINUITY
OF GOVERNMENT: Montana's Continuity in Government Act allows the Governor to relocate the
seat of government from Helena to an alternate location within the
boundaries of Montana, whether the necessity arises from enemy attack or
any other disaster. The Governor must choose other Montana cities in order
of their population. The cities of Billings, Great Falls, Butte, and
Missoula are designated in that order to become the new seat of government.

Montana has no plan for filling mass vacancies in state offices following a
catastrophe.

The Constitution provides that the Lieutenant Governor will serve as Acting
Governor when the Governor is so disabled that he is unable to communicate
his inability to perform the duties of office. However, when the
Lieutenant Governor and the Attorney General transmit to the state
legislature their written declaration that the Governor is unable to
discharge the powers and duties of the office, the legislature convenes to
determine the question of the Governor's inability. If the legislature,
within 21 days after convening, determines by a two-thirds vote of its
members that the Governor is, in fact, unable to discharge the powers and
duties of office, the Lieutenant Governor serves as Acting Governor.
Thereafter, when the Governor transmits to the legislature his own
declaration that no inability exists, he resumes the powers and duties of
the office within 15 days, unless the legislature determines otherwise by a
two-thirds vote of its members.

If the Governor and his or her three successors are killed in an enemy
attack, the senior member of the legislature acts as Governor.

Nebraska

DEFINITION: The Nebraska Disaster and Civil Defense Act of 1973 defines a disaster as the occurrence or imminent threat of widespread or severe damage, injury, or loss of life or property, resulting from any natural or manmade cause.

DECLARATION
OF EMERGENCY: The Governor may proclaim a state of disaster emergency, and may renew it after 30 days. The state of disaster emergency may be terminated at any time by either the Governor or the legislature. A civil defense emergency may only be proclaimed by the President, but may be terminated by the Governor or the legislature. Such an emergency takes effect automatically upon an attack on the United States.

GOVERNOR'S
EMERGENCY POWERS: During a disaster emergency, the Governor may suspend statutes regulating State business and all administrative laws as necessary, and may commandeer or utilize any private property, subject to compensation, as necessary. It is unclear whether the Governor has such powers during a civil defense emergency, although the conditions that give rise to such emergencies (such as enemy attack) allow the proclamation of a disaster emergency. The Governor generally may not interfere with labor disputes or the news media.

LEAD AGENCY: The Nebraska Civil Defense Agency is part of the Office of Adjutant General and is in charge of preparing, maintaining, and implementing a state disaster plan for all types of emergencies.

MUTUAL AID
AGREEMENTS: Nebraska is a member of the Interstate Civil Defense and Disaster Compact. The Governor is not authorized to enter into any other compacts.

PUBLIC/PERSONAL
LIABILITY: Persons who voluntarily allow the use of their premises as shelter for civil defense purposes are immune from liability. Civil defense workers, including volunteers, are generally immune from liability resulting from their actions.

CONTINUITY
OF GOVERNMENT: Each legislator is required to appoint three to seven "stand-by legislators" to succeed him or her in case of an enemy attack that annihilates the legislature. There are no provisions for other state offices.

The Nebraska statutes provide that if it appears the Governor is unable to perform the duties of office, a conference may be called by the individual next in line of succession of the office of the Governor--the Lieutenant Governor. The conference consists of the director of the Nebraska Psychiatric Institute, the dean of the College of Medicine of the University of Nebraska, and the dean of another accredited college of medicine located in the state. This three-member board examines the Governor and by unanimous vote and secret ballot may find the Governor incapable of discharging the duties of the office. The Governor must reconvene the conference in order to reverse the decision and may appeal to the Nebraska Supreme Court.

In the event of enemy attack, the Governor may remove the seat of government to any other location or locations.

Nevada

Chapter 414

DEFINITION: Nevada's emergency management statute covers disasters caused by hostile action or natural causes, but does not specifically address non-military manmade disasters. Disasters are events of unprecedented size and destructiveness that threaten the safety of Nevada inhabitants.

DECLARATION OF EMERGENCY: The Governor or the legislature may proclaim a state of emergency if an attack on the United States has occurred or is threatened, or a natural disaster of major proportions has actually occurred. The state of emergency lasts indefinitely until terminated by either the Governor or the legislature.

GOVERNOR'S EMERGENCY POWERS: The Governor is empowered to perform services for the purpose of emergency management on such terms and conditions as the Governor prescribes and without regard to the limitations of any existing law. The Governor is also authorized to procure any necessary materials for emergency management by any means, including condemnation and seizure (compensation must be provided for, however). The Governor's powers do not extend to most labor disputes or the dissemination of news.

LEAD AGENCY: The Division of Emergency Management is a unit of the Department of the Military and is responsible for preparing and implementing a program for emergency management. Nevada also has a Board of Search and Rescue which oversees programs for search and rescue activities among the Highway Patrol, the Civil Air Patrol, the National Guard, and other emergency organizations. The Board is appointed by the Director of Emergency Management.

MUTUAL AID AGREEMENTS: The Governor may enter into mutual aid arrangements with other states. Nevada is a member of the Interstate Civil Defense and Disaster Compact.

PUBLIC/PERSONAL LIABILITY: Volunteer and auxiliary workers are generally exempt from liability. Persons who allow their property to be used for shelter purposes are also generally immune.

LICENSING REQUIREMENTS: License requirements may be suspended for any authorized emergency worker.

CONTINUITY OF GOVERNMENT: The Nevada Constitution provides that the legislature shall have the power to provide for immediate and temporary succession to public offices in case of an enemy attack, and for relocation of the state capitol. The legislature has not provided for such emergency measures yet, however. Vacancies in the legislature are filled by the commissioners in the legislator's home county, who are to appoint successors from the same party.

New Hampshire

Chapter 107

DEFINITION:	New Hampshire's Civil Defense Act covers disasters that bring about the occurrence or threat of widespread or severe damage, injury, or loss of life or property resulting from any natural or manmade cause. A further policy of the state is to intervene only when the disaster is beyond local control.
DECLARATION OF EMERGENCY:	The Governor or the legislature may declare a state of civil defense emergency if an attack on the United States has occurred or is anticipated, or a natural disaster has actually occurred. The state of emergency may last indefinitely.
GOVERNOR'S EMERGENCY POWERS:	The Governor may perform services for civil defense purposes without regard to the limitations of existing law, and may seize certain private property, subject to compensation, including real estate, buildings, high explosives, transportation vehicles, food, clothing, or medicine in excess of the reasonable and immediate needs of the owner and his or her household, and fuel. The Governor may do this by specifying the type of property necessary within a general location. The Governor is not allowed to seize firearms or small arms ammunition.
LEAD AGENCY:	The Civil Defense Advisory Council consists of 18 members, drawn mostly from the government, and it advises the Governor on preparing and maintaining a state disaster plan. The State Civil Defense Agency has been delegated the Governor's authority to prepare and implement the disaster plan. The Civil Defense Agency is also in charge of preparing nuclear emergency response plans for each of the state's nuclear power plants. The New Hampshire State Port Authority is responsible for preventing contamination of the seacoast by oil or other substances.
MUTUAL AID AGREEMENTS:	The Governor may enter into mutual agreements with other states. New Hampshire is a member of the Interstate Civil Defense and Disaster Compact.
PUBLIC/PERSONAL LIABILITY:	Volunteer civil defense workers are generally immune from liability. Persons who voluntarily allow their property to be used as shelter are also generally immune.
LICENSING REQUIREMENTS:	Skilled persons may be authorized to practice without a license during an emergency.
CONTINUITY OF GOVERNMENT:	The Governor may declare an emergency temporary location for the seat of government due to any type of disaster, but the sites must be within New Hampshire. The Governor may convene the legislature elsewhere in case of any infectious distemper prevailing in the place where the legislature at any time is to convene. In case of an enemy attack that decimates state offices, each state officer has an emergency interim successor to take his or her place. Executive and legislative officers may designate three to five successors; the Governor designates three to five successors for all judicial officers.

New Jersey

DEFINITION: New Jersey's Civilian Defense and Disaster Control Act defines a disaster as any unusual incident resulting from natural or unnatural causes which endangers the health, safety, or resources of New Jersey inhabitants, and which is or may become too large or unusual to be handled in its entirety by regular municipal operating services.

DECLARATION
OF EMERGENCY: The Governor may proclaim a state of emergency if s/he deems it necessary. The state of emergency may last indefinitely until the Governor proclaims it to be at an end. The legislature is not authorized to end an emergency.

GOVERNOR'3
EMERGENCY POWERS: The Governor is authorized to temporarily employ, take, or use the personal services, or real and personal property of any citizen or resident of the state, or of any business as necessary. All orders, rules, and regulations issued by the Governor shall be binding upon each and every person within the state. The Governor may take possession and control of properties on the Atlantic Ocean or Delaware Bay ten days after (or sooner, if necessary) s/he finds the need to repair the protective barriers that are between a municipality and the water.

LEAD AGENCY: The Office of the Civilian Defense Director is part of the State Department of Defense, and is in charge of preparing and implementing a plan for coordinating civil defense. The Department of Environmental Protection is in charge of maintaining the State Radiation Emergency Response Plan.

MUTUAL AID
AGREEMENTS: The Governor is authorized to enter into mutual aid agreements with other states. New Jersey is a member of the Interstate Civil Defense and Disaster Compact.

PUBLIC/PERSONAL
LIABILITY: Volunteers who are reasonably attempting to comply with the orders of the Governor in an emergency are generally immune from liability. Persons who allow the use of their property as emergency shelter are also generally immune.

CONTINUITY
OF GOVERNMENT: In the threat of an enemy attack, the Governor may move the seat of government from Trenton to any other place. All executive officers shall designate three to seven emergency interim successors to take their places following a devastating enemy attack. There is no provision for judicial officers (vacancies to be filled by appointment or election) or legislators (vacancies filled by special election).

New Mexico

Chapter 12, Article 10

DEFINITION: New Mexico's State Civil Emergency Preparedness Act does not define emergencies or disasters, but covers disasters resulting from acts of war or sabotage, or from natural or manmade causes other than acts of war.

DECLARATION OF EMERGENCY: New Mexico does not provide for declaration of a state of emergency. The Governor may carry out a program for emergency operations whenever there is a disaster beyond local control.

GOVERNOR'S EMERGENCY POWERS: The Governor is empowered to issue, amend, or rescind the necessary orders, regulations, and procedures to carry out the provisions of the State Civil Emergency Preparedness Act. The orders are to be enforced by the political subdivisions of the State. New Mexico law does not specifically define what the Governor may order during an emergency, beyond directions given to government workers.

LEAD AGENCY: The Civil Emergency Preparedness Division of the Office of Military Affairs is in charge of preparing and carrying out a program for civil emergency preparedness.

MUTUAL AID AGREEMENTS: The Governor is authorized to enter into mutual aid agreements with other states. New Mexico has not enacted the Interstate Civil Defense and Disaster Compact into law.

PUBLIC/PERSONAL LIABILITY: Persons who voluntarily allow the use of their property for shelter purposes in an emergency are generally immune from liability. Civil defense workers are not exempted from liability by the New Mexico Emergency Act. However, state government and public employees acting within the scope of their duties are granted immunity from tort liability, and that immunity is not waived in the case of emergency workers.

CONTINUITY OF GOVERNMENT: In the event of enemy attack, provision is made for emergency successors to all state offices. The Governor designates three successors for all executive and judicial offices. The County Commission from each county designates five disaster successors for each legislator elected from that county. In the event of any type of disaster, the Governor may relocate the seat of government to any place if Santa Fe becomes unsafe.

New York

DEFINITION:

New York has laws dealing with two types of emergencies, enemy attacks and disasters. A disaster is the occurrence or imminent threat of widespread or severe damage, injury, or loss of life or property resulting from any natural or manmade causes.

DECLARATION
OF EMERGENCY:

Technically, New York has been in a state of defense emergency since April 12, 1951. This emergency is to end when a state of national emergency proclaimed in 1950 is officially terminated. In the event of an attack upon the United States, the State Civil Defense Commission may exercise emergency powers. The Governor may declare a state of disaster emergency that is to last no longer than six months, unless rescinded by the Governor sooner.

GOVERNOR'S
EMERGENCY POWERS:

During a disaster emergency, the Governor may temporarily suspend specific provisions of any law as necessary for up to 30 days, and may make such orders as are necessary to protect the public safety. Following an attack, the State Civil Defense Commission (and not the Governor) may take, use, or destroy any and all real or personal property as necessary, and may impress persons into service for the performance of emergency work (subject to compensation in both cases).

LEAD AGENCY:

The New York State Defense Council and the State Civil Defense Commission are in charge of establishing emergency programs to take effect in the event of enemy attack. The Council consists of 23 members who establish economic and conservation plans in case of an attack. The Commission consists of 21 members in charge of procuring emergency resources and providing for civil defense plans.

The Disaster Preparedness Commission consists of 20 members in charge of preparing and implementing state disaster preparedness plans. The members of all three Commissions are drawn from the directors of state agencies. The agencies carry out the provisions of the emergency plans.

MUTUAL AID
AGREEMENTS:

New York has enacted the Interstate Civil Defense and Disaster Compact into law.

PUBLIC/PERSONAL
LIABILITY:

Persons who are conscripted into emergency service after an attack are generally immune from liability. Authorized civil defense workers are also generally immune from liability. New York has a Good Samaritan law that applies to licensed physicians who render emergency aid, but not to private persons. New York does not provide an exemption from liability for property owners who allow their premises to be used as shelter.

CONTINUITY
OF GOVERNMENT:

After a disaster or an enemy attack, the legislature is empowered and required to provide for continuity of government operations. New York law does not require the seat of government to be in Albany at all times.

North Carolina

DEFINITION: The North Carolina Emergency Management Act of 1977 defines a disaster as an occurrence or imminent threat of widespread or severe damage, injury, or loss of life or property resulting from any natural or manmade accidental, military, or paramilitary cause.

DECLARATION OF EMERGENCY: An emergency may be declared by either the Governor or the General Assembly and may be terminated by either. The state of disaster lasts for an indefinite period of time.

GOVERNOR'S EMERGENCY POWERS: The Governor may procure materials and facilities for emergency management by any means, including seizure of private property, without regard to the limitation of any existing law, subject to compensation. The Governor may waive a provision of any regulation or ordinance of a state agency or a local governmental unit which restricts the immediate relief of human suffering, and may establish economic controls over all resources, materials, and services. However, the Governor may not interfere with the dissemination of news.

LEAD AGENCY: The Department of Crime Control and Public Safety is in charge of preparing and implementing the State Emergency Management Program.

MUTUAL AID AGREEMENTS: The Governor is authorized to enter into agreements for mutual aid with other states.

PUBLIC/PERSONAL LIABILITY: Persons who own real and personal property and who, voluntarily or involuntarily, knowingly or unknowingly, with or without compensation, allow it to be used for the purpose of sheltering or protecting any persons in an emergency shall not be civilly liable for torts arising from its use under any circumstances. Volunteer emergency management workers are generally immune from liability.

LICENSING REQUIREMENTS: Authorized emergency management workers who possess skills may practice those skills without a license in an emergency.

CONTINUITY OF GOVERNMENT: Although North Carolina has emergency provisions for continuity of local government, there are no similar provisions for state offices. Vacancies in the legislature are filled by gubernatorial appointment, with the recommendation of the county executive committee of the political party and county with which the vacating member was affiliated. Vacancies in other offices are also filled by the Governor. The Constitution permanently fixes the seat of government at Raleigh, and there are no provisions for it to be moved elsewhere.

The Constitution provides that the Governor may, by a written statement filed with the Attorney General, declare that he is physically incapable of performing the duties of the office and may, in the same manner, declare when he is physically capable of performing those duties. However, the mental incapacity of the Governor may be determined only by a joint resolution adopted by a vote of two-thirds of all members in each house of the General Assembly. In any event, the Assembly must notify the Governor and give him an opportunity to be heard before a joint session of the body before it takes final action. When the Assembly is not in session, a majority of the members of the Council of State (comprised of the other executive officers in the state--the Lieutenant Governor, Secretary of State, Auditor, Treasurer, Superintendent of Public Instruction, Attorney General, Commissioner of Agriculture, Commissioner of Labor, and Commissioner of Insurance) may convene the Assembly in extra session for the purpose of proceeding with the determination.

North Dakota

DEFINITION: The North Dakota Disaster Act of 1973 defines a disaster as the occurrence or imminent threat of widespread or severe damage, injury, or loss of life resulting from any natural or manmade cause.

DECLARATION
OF EMERGENCY: The Governor may declare a state of disaster emergency, but it is to last no more than 30 days unless renewed by the Governor. The legislature or the Governor may end the state of disaster emergency at any time.

GOVERNOR'S
EMERGENCY POWERS: The Governor may suspend the provisions regulatory of the conduct of state business and any administrative laws if necessary. S/he may also commandeer and utilize any private property as necessary, subject to compensation for the owners. The Governor may not, however, interfere with the dissemination of news and comment, nor interfere with a labor dispute except where necessary to protect public safety.

LEAD AGENCY: The Division of Disaster Emergency Services is part of the Office of the Adjutant General. The Division is in charge of preparing and maintaining a state disaster plan and implementing the plan in times of disaster.

MUTUAL AID
AGREEMENTS: The Governor may enter into mutual aid agreements with neighboring states and Canadian provinces if s/he finds that a vulnerable area lies only partly within North Dakota.

PUBLIC/PERSONAL
LIABILITY: Property owners who voluntarily allow their premises to be used for emergency purposes are generally immune from liability. Volunteer civil defense workers also are generally immune.

LICENSING
REQUITREMENTS: Skilled persons who are authorized emergency workers may practice without a license.

CONTINUITY
OF GOVERNMENT: The Governor may, in the face of an enemy attack, move the seat of government from Bismarck to any other place. All executive officers must designate three to seven emergency interim successors for themselves. The Governor designates successors for the Supreme Court, and the senior judge of each judicial circuit in the state designates at least three emergency judges for the lower courts. All legislators designate three to seven emergency successors for themselves. If the Governor and all of his or her constitutional successors are killed or rendered incapacitated, the office devolves upon the most recent former Governor (except for those serving in Congress).

Ohio

DEFINITION: Ohio's civil defense law covers attacks and natural and manmade disasters, and includes any phenomenon or act of man which creates a condition of emergency beyond the capability of the affected local government to control and resolve the incident, and any imminent threat of widespread and severe damage, personal injury or hardship, or loss of life or property.

DECLARATION
OF EMERGENCY: Ohio law has many references to the fact that the Governor may proclaim a state of emergency, but does not provide any details about the duration of emergency or the procedures for ending it. The Governor has power to suppress insurrection, to repel invasion, and to act in the event of a disaster within the state.

GOVERNOR'S
EMERGENCY POWERS: Ohio law is extremely vague concerning the powers of the Governor in an emergency. The Governor may promulgate regulations with respect to civil defense which may take effect during an emergency. The Governor may issue such orders as are necessary to minimize the effects upon the civilian population caused or which would be caused by an attack or other disaster. The Governor is not authorized to order the seizure of private property, nor is s/he directly authorized to suspend any existing laws. A violation of the Governor's emergency orders is punishable by up to a $50 fine and 60 days in prison.

LEAD AGENCY: The Disaster Services Agency is part of the Office of the Adjutant General and is in charge of preparing and coordinating all civil defense activities. An 11-member Disaster Services Advisory Council advises the Governor on emergency matters. The Emergency Medical Services Advisory Council is in charge of preparing a plan for emergency medical services during a disaster. The plan is to be implemented by the Disaster Services Agency.

MUTUAL AID
AGREEMENTS: The Governor may enter into mutual aid arrangements with other states. Ohio has not enacted the Interstate Civil Defense and Disaster Compact into law, but is a member of a mutual aid compact with Kentucky and West Virginia that takes effect in cases of enemy attack.

PUBLIC/PERSONAL
LIABILITY: Although Ohio encourages the construction of civil defense shelters through tax incentives, the state apparently does not immunize property owners from liability. Ohio does have a Good Samaritan statute that allows persons to render emergency care without fear of incurring civil liability.

CONTINUITY
OF GOVERNMENT: All executive officers shall appoint emergency interim successors for themselves. Vacancies in the General Assembly are filled by election by the members of the Senate or House who are of the same political party as the departed member. Columbus is the permanent seat of government. Although the Governor is not given authority to convene the legislature elsewhere, there is no requirement that the legislature meet at the seat of government.

Oklahoma

Title 63, Chapter 24

DEFINITION:

Oklahoma's civil defense laws provide for a state of emergency when an attack upon the United States has occurred or is imminent, or when a natural or manmade disaster has occurred.

DECLARATION
OF EMERGENCY:

The Governor, the legislature, or the President of the United States may proclaim a civil defense emergency if the United States has been attacked. The Governor may also declare a state of disaster emergency. If the Governor declares a civil defense emergency when attack has not actually occurred, or if s/he terminates such an emergency, the action must be approved by the legislature. A disaster emergency may be terminated by either the Governor or the legislature. Neither emergency proclamation may last longer than 30 days unless renewed unilaterally by the Governor or by the legislature.

GOVERNOR'S
EMERGENCY POWERS:

The Governor may issue orders, rules, and regulations to prevent and relieve emergencies, and assume direct operational control over civil defense activities. Although Oklahoma amended its Civil Defense Act in 1979 to include non-military disasters, it has not amended the law to give the Governor emergency powers that apply in situations where the United States has not been attacked. By law, the Governor has the power only during the existence of a civil defense emergency to activate the Oklahoma Emergency Resources Management Plan, assume direct control over all civil defense forces, and to provide for evacuation of the population. Oklahoma also does not provide for the seizure of property during an emergency, nor for the suspension of laws in an emergency.

LEAD AGENCY:

The Department of Civil Defense is responsible for preparing and implementing the program for civil defense. The Department of Emergency Resources Management has been in charge of preparing an emergency plan (which was implemented by the Civil Defense Agency), but that department is to continue only until July 1, 1984 in accordance with the Oklahoma Sunset Law.

The Civil Defense Advisory Council is composed of seven members who advise the Governor and the Director of Civil Defense on all matters pertaining to both types of emergencies. The seven members are all cabinet officials.

MUTUAL AID
AGREEMENTS:

The Governor may enter into mutual aid agreements with other states. Oklahoma has not enacted the Interstate Civil Defense and Disaster Compact into law.

PUBLIC/PERSONAL
LIABILITY:

Persons who allow their premises to be used for shelter purposes are generally exempt from liability. Volunteer emergency workers, whose services have been accepted by a proper authority, are generally immune from liability.

CONTINUITY
OF GOVERNMENT:

All executive officers and legislators must designate three to seven emergency successors. The Governor designates emergency judges for the Supreme Court and Court of Criminal Appeals, and the Chief Justice designates successors for the lower courts. The Governor may be succeeded by members of the State Highway Commission in the order of their numerical districts if his or her first eight successors are unavailable. The Governor may relocate the seat of government to any other location after any type of disaster if necessary; the succession acts apply only in case of enemy attack.

Oregon

DEFINITION: The Oregon Civil Defense Act of 1949 defines a disaster as the occurrence or imminent threat of widespread or severe damage, or loss of life or property resulting from any natural or manmade cause.

DECLARATION OF EMERGENCY: Oregon does not describe the Governor's powers in terms of declaring a state of emergency. Rather, when the Governor finds that an emergency exists in any area, s/he defines the boundaries of that area in writing, and designates it as an emergency disaster area. When the emergency is over, the Governor may proclaim the emergency disaster area to be dissolved.

If the United States has been attacked, or is in imminent danger of being attacked, the Governor may proclaim an emergency, which may not last longer than six months, after which any new proclamation must be renewed by the Governor with the concurrence of the legislature. The legislature may terminate an emergency proclamation at any time, and the Supreme Court may review the facts upon which the emergency was proclaimed, and decide whether the proclamation was warranted (Oregon is unique in permitting Court participation).

GOVERNOR'S EMERGENCY POWERS: After an enemy attack, the Governor may restrict the use of necessary resources such as food, fuel, clothing, and services, by ordering price-fixing, rationing, conservation, and other measures. The Governor's orders have the full force and effect of law. During a non-military emergency, the Governor may make orders and do all things deemed advisable and necessary to alleviate the immediate conditions, but s/he is not allowed specifically to commandeer private property or suspend existing laws.

LEAD AGENCY: The Emergency Management Division is charged with coordinating the activities of all civil defense organizations in the state, and carrying out the program for civil defense. The Division is advised by the 12-member Emergency Management Advisory Council, of which only two members are not state officers.

The Oregon Nuclear Emergency Organization is in charge of preparing an Emergency Resources Management Plan for implementation after an enemy attack upon the United States.

MUTUAL AID AGREEMENTS: The Governor is authorized to enter into agreements with other states. Oregon has not enacted the Interstate Civil Defense and Disaster Compact into law.

PUBLIC/PERSONAL LIABILITY: Persons who allow the use of their premises for shelter purposes are generally immune from liability. All civil defense workers, including volunteers, are generally immune from liability.

LICENSING REQUIREMENTS: Persons licensed in other states may practice in Oregon during an emergency without a license.

CONTINUITY OF GOVERNMENT: Oregon has no provision for relocating the government during an emergency; the Constitution requires any meetings of the legislature in the event of an emergency to be at the State Capital. Successors to legislative seats shall be nominated by the precinct committeepersons of the party representing the precincts within the district who were precinct committeepersons of the precinct when the vacancy occurred. The committeepersons shall nominate five qualified persons, and the county courts and commissioners shall elect one of the five people. Oregon has no emergency interim succession acts.

A 1959 statute provides that if the Governor is unable to perform his duties, either the Chief Justice of the state's Supreme Court or the individual next in line of succession to the office of the Governor—the Secretary of State—may call a conference. The conference participants include the Chief Justice, the Superintendent of the state hospital, and the dean of the University of Oregon Medical School. The conference, by secret ballot and unanimous vote, may find the Governor temporarily unable to fulfill the duties of his office.

Pennsylvania

Title 35, Chapters 71 and 73

DEFINITION: Pennsylvania's Emergency Management Services Code defines a disaster emergency as those conditions which may be found to seriously affect the safety, health, or welfare of a substantial number of citizens of the Commonwealth; be of such magnitude or severity as to render essential state supplementation of county and local efforts; and have been caused by forces beyond the control of man.

DECLARATION OF EMERGENCY: The Governor may proclaim and terminate a state of disaster emergency when the conditions listed above have occurred or are imminent. A state of disaster emergency shall not last more than 90 days unless renewed by the Governor. The General Assembly may terminate the state of disaster emergency at any time.

GOVERNOR'S EMERGENCY POWERS: The Governor may suspend the provisions of any regulatory statute prescribing procedures for the conduct of Commonwealth business, and any administrative laws. The Governor may commandeer or utilize private property as necessary, subject to compensation requirements. The Governor may not normally interfere in the course of a labor dispute, but interference with the dissemination of news and comment is not prohibited.

LEAD AGENCY: The Pennsylvania Emergency Management Agency is in charge of preparing and implementing a Pennsylvania Emergency Management Plan. The agency is advised by the Pennsylvania Emergency Management Council, which is comprised of 16 members (12 cabinet members and four legislators), but five members constitute a quorum.

MUTUAL AID AGREEMENTS: Pennsylvania has enacted the Interstate Civil Defense and Disaster Compact into law. The Governor is not authorized to enter into other compacts.

PUBLIC/PERSONAL LIABILITY: Employees and agents of the Commonwealth are generally immune from liability when they are performing duties pursuant to orders of the Governor. Pennsylvania repealed its law encouraging persons to allow their property to be used for emergency shelter in 1978.

CONTINUITY OF GOVERNMENT: Pennsylvania enacted emergency interim succession acts in 1959 for executive and judicial officers, and for legislative officers. All executive officers must designate at least three emergency interim successors to take their places after an attack. After an attack, the Governor may fill vacancies on the Supreme Court, and the Chief Justice may fill vacancies in the lower courts by appointing emergency judges.

After an attack, all surviving legislators convene within 90 days at the place where the Governor has his or her office. If the positions of Speaker of the House and/or President Pro Tempore of the Senate are vacant, the survivors elect persons from among them to serve. The Speaker and the President then appoint qualified persons as successors for absent senators and representatives. The successors assume the powers and duties, but not the offices, of the absent legislators.

Rhode Island

DEFINITION: The Rhode Island Defense Civil Preparedness Act defines a disaster as the occurrence or imminent threat of widespread or severe damage, injury, or loss of life or property resulting from any natural or manmade cause requiring emergency action to avert danger or damage. Rhode Island's act covers all disasters, including volcanic activity.

DECLARATION OF EMERGENCY: The Governor may declare an emergency for not more than 30 days unless renewed by him or her. The state of emergency may be terminated by the Governor or by the General Assembly at any time.

GOVERNOR'S EMERGENCY POWERS: The Governor may suspend any statute regulating the conduct of state business, or any administrative laws, if necessary. The Governor may commandeer and utilize any private property as necessary, subject to compensation. The Governor may designate a special emergency health and sanitation area for any part of the state which has increased suddenly in population due to disaster, and create emergency health regulations for the area. Finally, if the Governor foresees a serious shortage of food, fuel, clothing, or other resources, s/he may impose economic controls to prevent waste, hoarding, or profiteering.

LEAD AGENCY: The Defense Civil Preparedness Agency is in charge of preparing, maintaining, and coordinating a comprehensive plan and program for disasters. The Rhode Island Defense Civil Preparedness Advisory Council is in charge of reviewing all emergency programs in the State and advises the Governor during emergencies. Members are paid $25.00 per meeting. The Council consists of 11 members drawn from the Governor's cabinet, and 11 representatives appointed by the Governor from the legislature, public utilities, the general public, the Rhode Island Petroleum Association, and the Rhode Island League of Cities and Towns. The Advisory Council was originally to have been eliminated by July 1983, but is currently operating under a renewal of authority.

MUTUAL AID AGREEMENTS: The Governor may cooperate with the officials of other states in formulating common disaster plans. Rhode Island's membership in the Interstate Civil Defense and Disaster Compact limits the Governor to making agreements with bordering states.

PUBLIC/PERSONAL LIABILITY: Volunteer disaster response workers are generally immune from liability, as the persons who allow their premises to be used as shelter for emergency purposes.

LICENSING REQUIREMENTS: Authorized disaster response workers may practice without a license in an emergency.

CONTINUITY OF GOVERNMENT: The Governor may remove the seat of government from Providence to any other location in the face of an enemy attack. Rhode Island has no emergency provisions to fill mass vacancies in state offices following a catastrophe. The Governor fills most offices by appointment, and legislative seats must be filled by special election.

South Carolina

Title 25, Chapter 1, Article 4

DEFINITION: South Carolina defines an emergency as actual or threatened enemy attack, sabotage, conflagration, flood, storm, epidemic, earthquake, riot, or other public calamity.

DECLARATION OF EMERGENCY: The Governor may declare a state of emergency which shall not continue for more than 15 days without the consent of the General Assembly.

GOVERNOR'S EMERGENCY POWERS: The Governor may suspend the provisions of statutes regulatory of the conduct of state business if necessary (no specific provision for suspending all of the rules, regulations, and orders issued by state agencies). The Governor is not authorized to seize private property during an emergency. All proclamations of the Governor during an emergency shall have the force and effect of law.

LEAD AGENCY: The South Carolina Emergency Preparedness Division is part of the Office of the Adjutant General and is in charge of developing and implementing a State Emergency Plan.

MUTUAL AID AGREEMENTS: South Carolina has entered into the Interstate Civil Defense and Disaster Compact.

PUBLIC/PERSONAL LIABILITY: South Carolina has no provision in its emergency act exempting private persons from liability. However, its Good Samaritan law provides that any person who in good faith gratuitously renders emergency care at the scene of an accident, or emergency to a victim, shall not be liable for any civil damages, except for gross negligence or willful misconduct.

LICENSING REQUIREMENTS: Skilled professionals licensed in other states may render aid in times of emergency without a license.

CONTINUITY OF GOVERNMENT: All state executive officers shall designate three to seven emergency interim successors for themselves. The Governor designates emergency judges to succeed members of the Supreme Court. The Chief Justice designates successors for all courts of record, and the judges of each circuit court designate successors for all other courts. All members of the General Assembly designate three to seven emergency successors for themselves. The Governor may remove the seat of government from Columbia to any other location or locations if necessary.

Note: All emergency provisions apply only in cases of enemy attack.

South Dakota

Title 33, Chapter 33-15

DEFINITION:
South Dakota's Emergency Act applies generally to the occurrence (disaster) or threat (emergency) of any natural, nuclear, manmade, war-related, or other catastrophe, producing phenomena in any part of the state which could cause damage of such severity and magnitude that total state assistance is warranted.

DECLARATION OF EMERGENCY:
The Governor may declare a state of emergency or a disaster that lasts indefinitely. South Dakota law does not provide for the termination of a state of emergency.

GOVERNOR'S EMERGENCY POWERS:
The Governor is not afforded any specific powers under South Dakota law. In an emergency or disaster, s/he may assume direct operational control over all or any part of the emergency and disaster functions within the state. The Governor may also call upon and use any facilities and equipment available from any source as necessary, but the law does not provide for compensation to owners. The Governor and/or the Adjutant General are authorized to make orders, rules, and regulations as necessary.

LEAD AGENCY:
The Division of Emergency and Disaster Services is part of the Office of the Adjutant General (also called the Department of Military and Veteran Affairs), and is in charge of preparing and coordinating a comprehensive program for emergency and disaster service. The Adjutant General is responsible for the activities of the division.

MUTUAL AID AGREEMENTS:
The Adjutant General and the directors of local emergency organizations may enter into mutual aid arrangements with other states, or other states' agencies, subject to the approval of the Governor. As of 1983, South Dakota had not enacted the Interstate Civil Defense and Disaster Compact into law.

PUBLIC/PERSONAL LIABILITY:
Persons who allow their premises to be used as shelter for civil defense purposes in connection with enemy attack, and not for shelter during non-military emergencies, are generally immune from liability. Volunteer disaster service workers are generally immune from liability.

LICENSING REQUIREMENTS:
Authorized emergency and disaster service workers may practice skills without a license in an emergency.

CONTINUITY OF GOVERNMENT:
In the face of an enemy attack, the Governor may order the seat of government removed from Pierre to any other location or locations. All state and local officers must designate emergency interim successors to follow them. Judges may designate their own successors. Legislators may also designate three to seven successors, and if they fail to do so, the party leader in their house shall do so.

Tennessee

Title 58, Chapter 2

DEFINITION:

Tennessee defines an emergency as the threat or actual occurrence of a disaster that is of sufficient severity and magnitude to warrant disaster assistance by the state. Disasters are conditions that threaten or cause substantial damage to property, human suffering, hardship or loss of life.

DECLARATION OF EMERGENCY:

The Governor may declare a state of emergency, or, if s/he is unavailable, the Adjutant General may do so. The state of emergency lasts indefinitely until terminated by the Governor.

GOVERNOR'S EMERGENCY POWERS:

The Governor may seize private property for the protection of the public, including all means of transportation and communication (no exemption for the news media); all energy resources in accordance with plans prepared by the Division of Energy of the Department of Economic and Community Development; food, clothing, equipment, and supplies; and buildings and plants. Compensation to owners must be provided in event of loss or damage. The Governor's orders may supersede existing laws if the orders impose heavier restrictions than existing laws. Violation of the Governor's orders is a misdemeanor and may be punished by up to six months in prison and a $500 fine. All state employees are subject to being assigned to mobile reserve units in the event of an emergency.

LEAD AGENCY:

The Tennessee Emergency Management Agency is part of the Department of the Military, and is in charge of creating and carrying out a program for civil defense.

MUTUAL AID AGREEMENTS:

The Governor may enter into mutual aid agreements with the several contiguous states. Tennessee has passed the Interstate Civil Defense and Disaster Compact into law.

PUBLIC/PERSONAL LIABILITY:

Persons who voluntarily allow the use of their premises for any civilian defense purpose are generally immune from liability. Volunteers are not exempted from liability by the Civil Defense Act, but are immune under Tennessee's Good Samaritan law.

CONTINUITY OF GOVERNMENT:

Tennessee has no provision for filling mass vacancies in state offices following a catastrophe. The county legislative body, i.e., county commissioners, may elect an interim successor for a vacant legislative seat until the seat can be filled in a special general election. The General Assembly may, in cases of overriding and controlling emergency, assemble and convene temporarily at some place in the state other than the seat of government. This is a rule drawn from Frierson v. General Assembly of Presbyterian Church, 54 Tenn. 683 (1872).

Texas

Article 6889-7

DEFINITION:
The Texas Disaster Act of 1975 defines a disaster as the occurrence or imminent threat of widespread or severe damage, injury, or loss of life or property resulting from any natural or manmade cause. An energy emergency is a temporary shortage of petroleum or liquid fuel energy supplies anywhere in the state.

DECLARATION OF EMERGENCY:
The Governor may declare a state of emergency which is not to last longer than 30 days, unless s/he renews it. The Governor or the legislature may terminate the emergency at any time.

GOVERNOR'S EMERGENCY POWERS:
The Governor may suspend the provisions of any regulatory statute prescribing the conduct of state business, and any administrative laws, if necessary. The Governor may commandeer or utilize any private property as necessary, subject to compensation. However, the Governor may not unreasonably interfere in a labor dispute, nor may s/he interfere with the dissemination of news and comment. The Governor may not authorize the removal of debris or wreckage from any property until the property owner gives unconditional authorization to do so.

LEAD AGENCY:
The State Division of Emergency Management is in charge of preparing, maintaining, and coordinating a comprehensive state emergency plan. A Disaster Emergency Funding Board is responsible for maintaining a disaster contingency fund so that funds to meet disasters will always be available. The Board is composed of five members--the Governor, Lieutenant Governor, and the directors of the State Board of Insurance, the Department of Human Resources, and the Division of Emergency Services. The Governor may establish an Emergency Management Council for advice on emergency preparedness, but is not obligated to do so.

MUTUAL AID AGREEMENTS:
Texas enacted the Interstate Civil Defense and Disaster Compact in 1951. In 1977, Texas abolished the office of the ICDDC Administrator, and provided that the Act expires effective September 1, 1987.

PUBLIC/PERSONAL LIABILITY:
Texas is one of the few states that does not encourage people to allow their premises to be used for shelter purposes by exempting the property owners from liability. However, Texas' Good Samaritan law allows persons to render aid without fear of liability.

LICENSING REQUIREMENTS:
Skilled professionals licensed in other states may render aid without a license.

CONTINUITY OF GOVERNMENT:
All executive branch officers are required to designate three to seven persons to succeed them in the event of attack. The executive director of the state Employees Retirement System is to submit to the Lieutenant Governor and Speaker of the House three to seven names of former legislators from each district. The Lieutenant Governor and Speaker of the House are to contact each former Senator and Representative, respectively, and determine their willingness to serve as emergency interim successors. As a back-up to the list, each legislator is entitled to designate three to seven interim successors of the same political party. Each designee must meet the legal qualifications for the legislative office they must fill. If in the event of attack a legislator is unavailable, the Secretary of State is to notify the interim successor of the time and place of the legislative session. The interim successor exercises the same powers and duties of the legislator s/he succeeds, but may not designate a successor. In the event of an attack, the quorum requirements for the legislature are suspended, and if the required vote of a specified proportion of members is ordinarily required for approval, the same proportion of those present and voting is to be sufficient for its passage.

Utah

Title 63, Chapter 5

DEFINITION:
Utah defines a disaster as a situation causing or threatening to cause widespread damage, social disruption, or injury, or loss of life or property resulting from attack, internal disturbance, natural phenomena, or technological hazard.

DECLARATION
OF EMERGENCY:
The Governor may proclaim a state of emergency, and the legislature or the Governor may terminate it at any time. No state of emergency may last longer than 30 days unless renewed by joint resolution of the legislature. A state of emergency with regard to energy resources may last up to 60 days, and is renewable by the Governor or by the legislature, and may only be ended by the Governor.

GOVERNOR'S
EMERGENCY POWERS:
The Governor may temporarily suspend any public health, safety, zoning, transportation, or other requirement of the law or regulation, as necessary, in order to provide temporary housing to disaster victims. The Governor may suspend the provisions of any administrative law as necessary, and his orders have the effect of law, as long as they do not conflict with existing statutes. The Governor may purchase or lease public or private property for public use. The implication of this provision is that private property may be taken during an emergency, and purchased or leased later. In an energy emergency, the Governor may exercise all these powers and may order conservation of energy resources.

LEAD AGENCY:
The Division of Comprehensive Emergency Management is part of the Department of Public Safety, and is in charge of preparing, implementing, and maintaining all state emergency management plans. The Disaster Emergency Advisory Council is comprised of 18 members, drawn mostly from state cabinet officers, and is in charge of advising the Governor during an emergency.

MUTUAL AID
AGREEMENTS:
The Governor is authorized to enter into interstate agreements for mutual aid. Utah is a member of the Interstate Civil Defense and Disaster Compact, along with 12 other western states, and the Western Interstate Nuclear Compact.

PUBLIC/PERSONAL
LIABILITY:
Persons who allow their premises to be used as shelter for civil defense puprposes are generally immune from liability. Persons who assist in emergency activities, if authorized, are considered to be uncompensated employees of the state and generally may not be sued.

CONTINUITY
OF GOVERNMENT:
The disability of the Governor may be determined under the Constitution, either by the Governor's written declaration to the state Supreme Court of his inability to discharge the powers and duties of the office, or by a majority of the Supreme Court on joint request of the President Pro Tempore of the Senate and the Speaker of the House of Representatives. Thereafter, the Governor must transmit to the Court a written declaration to the contrary, unless, upon joint request of the President and the Speaker or its own initiative, the Court determines that the Governor is unable to discharge the powers and duties of the office. The Supreme Court has exclusive jurisdiction in the matter of gubernatorial disability.

Utah voters approved a Constitutional amendment in 1960 to allow for the passage of acts providing for an Emergency Seat of Government, Emergency Interim Executive and Judicial Succession, and Emergency Interim Legislative Succession. However, the amendment was declared ineffective, and the acts were declared unconstitutional because of a technicality in the 1960 election. The issue was not brought before the voters again, and Utah currently has no emergency provisions for continuity of government in times of emergency.

Vermont

Title 20

DEFINITION:

Vermont's civil defense laws cover disasters or emergencies of unprecedented size and destructiveness resulting from hostile action or from natural causes. Radiological incidents are specifically included in the definition of natural causes.

DECLARATION OF EMERGENCY:

The Governor may declare a state of emergency after the United States or Canada has been attacked and persons or property within the bounds of the state are affected, or after a natural disaster has occurred and the head municipal authority in a village, town, or city requests the Governor to declare an emergency. The Governor may terminate a natural disaster emergency at any time. S/he may terminate an enemy attack emergency only with the concurrence of a majority of the Civil Defense Board.

GOVERNOR'S EMERGENCY POWERS:

In an emergency, the Governor has the power to make orders to protect public health and safety, and has control over the resources and personnel of the state. In an attack, the Governor may exercise additional powers (with the concurrence of the Civil Defense Board), including the seizure of private property, subject to compensation of the owners. The Governor may seize all means of transportation, stocks of fuel, food, clothing, equipment, and buildings (but not homes).

LEAD AGENCY:

The Civil Defense Division of the Department of Public Safety is responsible for creating and implementing a civil defense program for the state. In the event of a war emergency, the Governor and the Civil Defense Board may establish a cabinet-level Civil Defense Agency that has the same powers and duties as the Civil Defense Division.

The Civil Defense Board is comprised of the Governor, the Lieutenant Governor, the Speaker of the House, and two members of the House appointed by him, and a member of the Senate appointed by the President of the Senate. The Board's members advise the Governor on emergency matters, and have certain powers in an emergency, including the expenditure of all funds allocated for emergency planning.

MUTUAL AID AGREEMENTS:

The Governor may enter into mutual aid compacts with other states. Vermont is a member of the Interstate Civil Defense and Disaster Compact.

PUBLIC/PERSONAL LIABILITY:

Persons who allow the use of their premises as shelter for civilian defense purposes (enemy attack) are generally immune from liability. Civil defense workers, including volunteers who are authorized, are also immune. Vermont's Good Samaritan law requires persons to be good samaritans. The law states that a person who knows that another is exposed to grave physical harm shall give reasonable assistance to the exposed person. Violation of the law is punishable by a fine of up to $100.

CONTINUITY OF GOVERNMENT:

All executive officers in the state are required to designate at least three emergency interim successors to fill in for them after an enemy attack. The Governor may appoint qualified persons to fill vacancies in the General Assembly, in which case s/he is to consider the recommendations of the state party organization, but is not bound to choose one of their nominees. The Governor may move the seat of government elsewhere if Montpelier becomes unsafe due to an enemy attack on the United States or Canada.

Virginia

DEFINITION:
The Commonwealth of Virginia Emergency Services and Disaster Law of 1973 defines an emergency as the threat or actual occurrence of a disaster in any part of the State of such disastrous severity or magnitude that governmental action beyond that authorized or contemplated by existing law is required because governmental inaction would work immediate and irrevocable harm upon the citizens of the Commonwealth.

DECLARATION
OF EMERGENCY:
The Governor may declare a state of emergency as necessary, and it may last indefinitely. However, any orders or rules promulgated by the Governor according to a state emergency plan do not have any effect beyond the June 30th following the next adjournment of the regular session of the General Assembly.

GOVERNOR'S
EMERGENCY POWERS:
The Governor may issue orders that have the full force and effect of law in order to control the use of food, fuel, clothing, services, and other necessities. Each member of the General Assembly must receive a copy of all emergency orders issued by the Governor. The Governor is not specifically authorized to seize private property for emergency use.

LEAD AGENCY:
The State Office of Emergency Services is part of the Department of Transportation, and is in charge of preparing, maintaining, and administering a State Emergency Operations Plan. During an emergency, the Governor is Director of Emergency Services and has full control over the office.

MUTUAL AID
AGREEMENTS:
The Governor may enter into mutual aid arrangements with other states. Virginia has not formally enacted the Interstate Civil Defense and Disaster Compact into law.

PUBLIC/PERSONAL
LIABILITY:
Any person who allows the use of his or her premises for emergency purposes is generally immune from liability. Persons who gratuitously repair electronic devices or equipment for the Office of Emergency Services are immune from civil liability. Volunteer emergency workers are generally immune from liability for acts that arise from their duties.

LICENSING
REQUIREMENTS:
Persons licensed in other states may render emergency aid in Virginia.

CONTINUITY
OF GOVERNMENT:
The Constitution provides that the Governor may submit a written declaration of his or her inability to the President Pro Tempore of the Senate and the Speaker of the House of Delegates. However, the Attorney General, President Pro Tempore, and Speaker (or a majority of the total membership of the General Assembly) may transmit to the Clerks of each House their written declaration of the Governor's inability. Thereafter, the Governor must transmit a declaration of his ability to discharge the powers and duties and resume office, unless those same officials transmit, within four days, their declaration that the Governor is still unable to serve. In that case, the General Assembly, convening within 48 hours, decides the matter. If, within 21 days after receipt of the latter declaration, the Assembly determines by a three-fourths vote of the elected membership of each House that the Governor is unable to discharge the duties of office, the Lieutenant Governor becomes Governor.

Virginia does not have any provisions to fill vacancies in state government following a catastrophe. Vacancies in the General Assembly are filled by special election. The legislature sits at Richmond, but may adjourn to any other place. The Governor may also move the seat of government as necessary.

Washington

Titles 38, 42, 43

DEFINITION: Washington's emergency management laws allow an emergency to be declared in the face of public disorder, energy emergency (shortage of energy resources), riot, or disaster (hostile action or natural causes) of sufficient degree of destructiveness as to warrant state action.

DECLARATION OF EMERGENCY: The Governor may proclaim and terminate all states of emergency, and the state of emergency may last as long as necessary. However, Washington law provides that the Governor must terminate the state of emergency proclamation when order has been restored in the area affected. Energy emergencies terminate after 45 days unless extended.

GOVERNOR'S EMERGENCY POWERS: The Governor may issue orders to restrict movement on public streets and highways, and the possession, distribution, and sale of commodities that s/he reasonably believes should be prohibited to help preserve and maintain life, health, property, or the public peace. During an energy emergency, the Governor may exercise these powers and order measures designed to conserve energy resources. During an emergency, the Governor and other local chief executives and emergency services directors have the power to command the service and equipment of as many citizens as considered necessary in the light of the disaster proclaimed, subject to compensation requirements.

LEAD AGENCY: The Department of Emergency Services is in charge of preparing and administering the state programs for emergency services and emergency assistance. The Emergency Services Council consists of seven to fifteen members appointed by the Governor who advise him/her on matters pertaining to emergencies.

MUTUAL AID AGREEMENTS: The Governor may enter into mutual aid arrangements with other states and Canadian provinces. Washington is a member of the Interstate Civil Defense and Disaster Compact.

PUBLIC/PERSONAL LIABILITY: Persons who allow their premises to be used for civil defense purposes are generally immune from liability. Persons performing services as emergency services workers are generally exempt from civil liability (this includes persons impressed into service during an emergency, and volunteers accepted to do emergency work).

LICENSING REQUIREMENTS: Skilled persons may be authorized to render aid without a license during an emergency.

CONTINUITY OF GOVERNMENT: In the event of enemy attack that decimates state offices, the surviving members of the legislature may meet at the place where the Governor is residing, and may pass laws regardless of quorum requirements, until the legislature can be filled by special elections. Appointed officers may designate temporary interim successors for themselves. In the face of an attack, the Governor may move the seat of government from Olympia to any location in Washington, Idaho, or Oregon.

53

West Virginia

DEFINITION:
West Virginia provides for the existence of a state of emergency when an attack on the United States or a natural or manmade disaster of major proportions has occurred or is imminent.

DECLARATION
OF EMERGENCY:
The Governor or the legislature may declare and terminate all states of emergency, whether by proclamation or by joint resolution. States of emergency may last indefinitely until termminated.

GOVERNOR'S
EMERGENCY POWERS:
The Governor may suspend the provisions of statutes regulating the conduct of state business, and any administrative laws as necessary. The Governor may procure materials and facilities for emergency services by condemnation and by seizure, if necessary, and s/he may obtain the services of necessary personnel. In both cases, compensation is required for lost property or services.

LEAD AGENCY:
The Office of Emergency Services is in charge of preparing and carrying out the state program for emergency services. The Emergency Services Advisory Council is in charge of advising the Governor and the Director of the OES on all matters pertaining to emergencies. The Council consists of seven members appointed by the Governor.

MUTUAL AID
AGREEMENTS:
The Governor may enter into mutual aid arrangements with other states. West Virginia is a member of the Interstate Civil Defense and Disaster Compact.

PUBLIC/PERSONAL
LIABILITY:
Duly qualified emergency service workers are generally immune from liability. Persons who allow their premises to be used as shelter in emergencies are also normally exempt from civil liability.

LICENSING
REQUIREMENTS:
Authorized emergency service workers may practice without a license.

CONTINUITY
OF GOVERNMENT:
All executive officers and legislators are required to designate three to seven emergency interim successors (if an individual legislator fails to designate a successor, his or her party leader may choose as many as necessary). Justices of the Supreme Court may designate emergency judges to succeed them. The lower court judges may not designate successors, but West Virginia has a unique provision—after a catastrophe, emergency interim judges may be elected by the attorneys in each county. If the constitutional successors to the Governor and the cabinet officers have been found unable to serve, resident ex-Governors succeed to the office in inverse order of service. The Governor may move the state capitol if faced with enemy attack.

Wisconsin

Chapter 166 (formerly Chapter 22)

DEFINITION: Wisconsin defines emergencies as situations resulting from enemy action and natural or manmade disasters.

DECLARATION OF EMERGENCY: The Governor may declare a state of emergency for the state or any portion thereof if s/he determines that an emergency resulting from enemy action or natural or manmade disaster exists. The duration of a state of emergency does not exceed 60 days if caused by enemy action, or 30 days if manmade or natural, but may be extended by joint resolution of the legislature. The proclamation may be revoked by the Governor or joint resolution of the legislature.

GOVERNOR'S EMERGENCY POWERS: During a state of emergency, the Governor may issue such orders as s/he deems necessary for the security of persons or property. The Governor may take, use, and destroy private property for government purposes. Wisconsin appears to be the only state that expressly allows the Governor to destroy private property in the name of the state. A claim may be made against the state for reimbursement.

LEAD AGENCY: The Secretary of the Department of Administration is responsible for developing, maintaining, and implementing a state emergency management plan.

MUTUAL AID AGREEMENTS: The Governor may enter into mutual aid agreements with other states.

PUBLIC/PERSONAL LIABILITY: Volunteer workers are indemnified by their sponsor against any civil liability incurred in the performance of emergency government activities while acting in good faith and in a reasonable manner. Persons who grant real estate that they own voluntarily to the state are not liable for deaths or injuries if they make known to the licensee any hidden dangers or safety hazards known to the owner or occupier of the premises.

CONTINUITY OF GOVERNMENT: The Governor shall proclaim an emergency temporary location for the seat of government as often as the exigencies of the situation require. All state officers may designate interim successors to their powers and duties. The Governor has the discretion to appoint a different successor. Vacancies in the legislature shall be filled by special election. Vacancies in the judicial offices may be filled by temporary appointment by the Governor until an election can be held.

Wyoming

Wyo. Stat. § 19-5

DEFINITION: The Wyoming Disaster and Civil Defense Act defines disasters as situations of unprecedented size and destructiveness resulting from enemy attack, sabotage, civil disorder, or other hostile action, or from natural causes. There is no provision for non-military manmade disasters.

DECLARATION OF EMERGENCY: The Governor may declare a state of emergency. There are no provisions as to the length of time or legislative termination of a state of emergency.

GOVERNOR'S EMERGENCY POWERS: The Governor may make, amend, and rescind the necessary orders, rules, and regulations to carry out the Disaster and Civil Defense Act.

LEAD AGENCY: The Disaster and Civil Defense Agency, a unit of the state Military Department, serves as the lead emergency management agency. The Disaster and Civil Defense Advisory Board is appointed by the Governor, with membership from representative citizens of commercial enterprises, service organizations, and public spirited groups.

MUTUAL AID AGREEMENTS: The Governor and disaster and civil defense coordinator may develop reciprocal disaster and civil defense aid arrangements for mutual aid with other political subdivisions.

PUBLIC/PERSONAL LIABILITY: Any disaster or civil defense worker reasonably attempting to comply with the law, or any order, rule, or regulation thereunder, is not liable for the death or injury to persons or for damage to property as a result of the activity or training. Any person who permits the use of any part of real estate for purposes of sheltering persons, during actual or mock exercises, is not civilly liable for negligence causing death, injury, or loss of property of any person.

LICENSING REQUIREMENTS: Licensing requirements may be suspended for emergency medical personnel who are licensed to practice in another state.

CONTINUITY OF GOVERNMENT: The Governor makes temporary appointments to fill a vacancy in any state office, other than the office of the Supreme Court Justice and the office of district court judge. A vacancy in the office of the Supreme Court or any district court shall be filled by appointment of the Governor. Legislative vacancies are filled by special election. The Wyoming Constitution grants the Governor the power to convene the legislature at a place other than the seat of government in times of grave emergency, as defined by law.

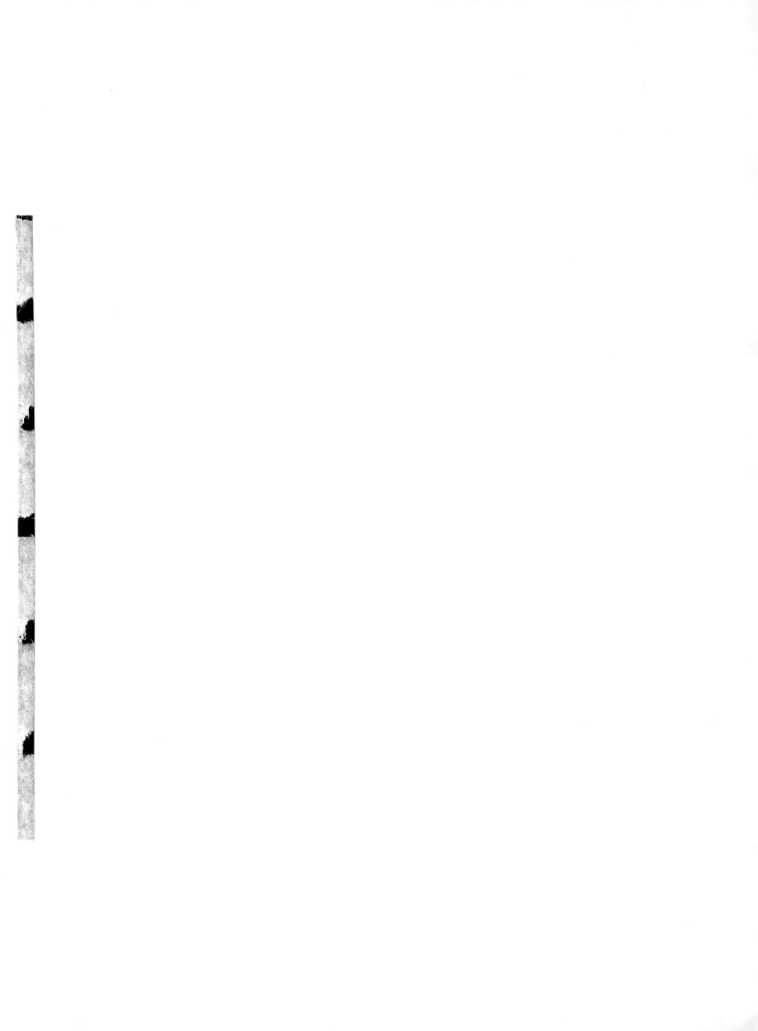

The Council of State Governments

The Council is a joint agency of all the state governments—created, supported, and directed by them. It conducts research on state programs and problems; maintains an information service available to state agencies, officials, and legislators; issues a variety of publications; assists in state-federal liaison; promotes regional and state-local cooperation; and provides staff for affiliated organizations.

HEADQUARTERS OFFICE
Iron Works Pike
P.O. Box 11910
Lexington, Kentucky 40578
(606) 252-2291

EASTERN OFFICE
1500 Broadway, 18th Floor
New York, New York 10036
(212) 221-3630

MIDWESTERN OFFICE
203 North Wabash Avenue
Chicago, Illinois 60601
(312) 236-4011

SOUTHERN OFFICE
3384 Peachtree Road, N.E.
Atlanta, Georgia 30326
(404) 266-1271

WESTERN OFFICE
720 Sacramento Street, 3rd Floor
San Francisco, California 94108
(415) 986-3760

WASHINGTON OFFICE
Hall of the States
444 North Capitol Street
Washington, D.C. 20001
(202) 624-5450